G000079743

**Sweet Art**

# CREATURE COOKIES

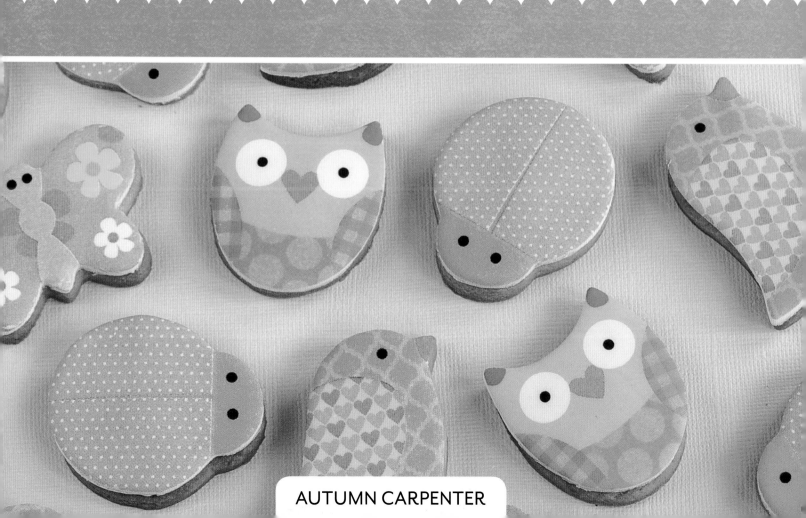

AUTUMN CARPENTER

**Creative Publishing**
**international**

Copyright © 2015 Creative Publishing international

All rights reserved. No part of this work covered by the copyrights hereon may be reproduced or used in any form or by any means—graphic, electronic, or mechanical, including photocopying, recording, or taping of information on storage and retrieval systems—without the written permission of the publisher.

Due to differing conditions, materials, and skill levels, the publisher and various manufacturers disclaim any liability for unsatisfactory results or injury due to improper use of tools, materials, or information in this publication.

First published in the United States of America by

Creative Publishing international, a division of
Quarto Publishing Group USA, Inc.
400 First Avenue North
Suite 400
Minneapolis, MN 55401

1-800-328-3895

www.creativepub.com

Visit www.Craftside.net for a behind-the-scenes peek at our crafty world!

ISBN: 978-1-58923-857-2

Digital edition published in 2015
eISBN: 978-1-62788-276-7

10 9 8 7 6 5 4 3 2 1

Library of Congress Cataloging-in-Publication Data available

Copy Editor: Karen Levy
Book Design, Page Layout and Illustrations: Mattie Wells
Photographs: Autumn Carpenter
Printed in China

Cookie decorating is my favorite hobby. Watching birds and critters in my backyard and visiting zoos are favorite pastimes. I've combined two of my passions to bring this book to life. Creating small, edible animals is delightful! As you meet these animals—from pets at home to critters in the ocean—you'll see that no two of them are identical. Each creature has his own personality that the icing or rolled fondant creates.

Decorating cookies doesn't involve a lot of expensive tools or ingredients: cookie cutters can be found in nearly every craft store, and icing ingredients are readily available. If you have decorated cookies before, I am confident you will be able to master all of the cookies in this book. If you are just beginning, read through the Basic Baking and Decorating section to understand the basic skills of cookie decorating. This section is also where you will find my tried-and-true recipes for cookies and icings. Before you begin, make sure you understand the different types of icings and how to use them. There are a lot of simple but important instructions and tips. Then, get started and employ those skills to decorate your first cookies. You will be pleasantly surprised at how easy and rewarding it is!

The step-by-step instructions will guide you to create the cookies as pictured, but I hope you are inspired to explore your own imagination. Change the colors of the creatures, use a different cookie cutter, or simply use the projects as a starting point for your own interpretation. Whether you are a new decorator or a pro, before long, you'll have an assortment of creature cookies to delight. I'm thrilled to share my animal cookies and hope you are enthused to create your own.

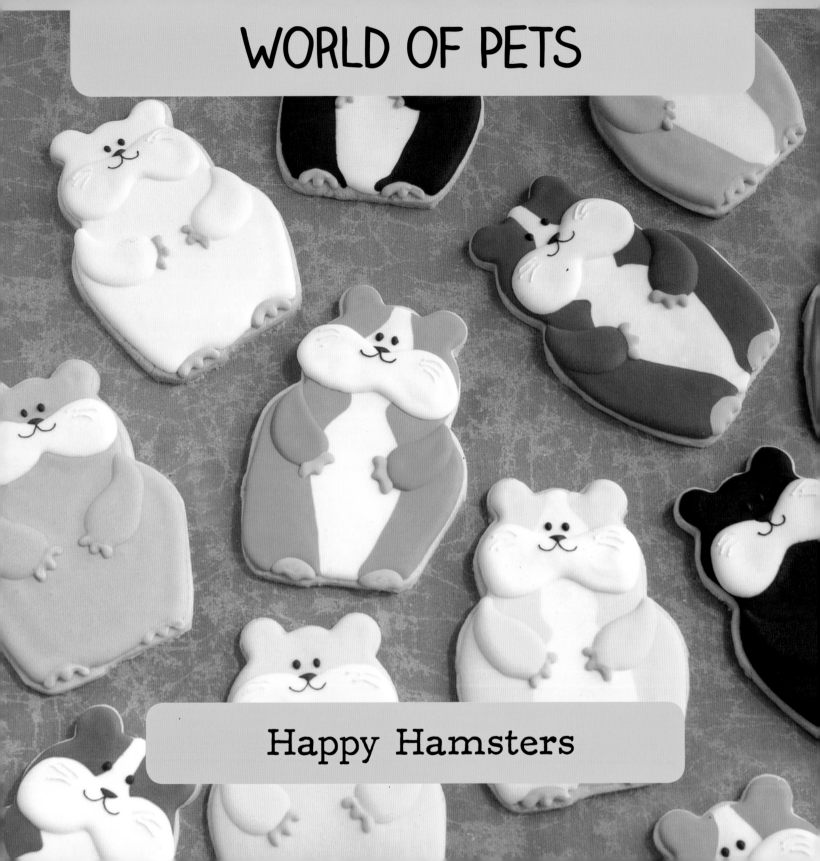

Happy Hamsters

## Techniques

Trimming the Cut Cookie Dough
  (pg. 118)

Run Sugar Icing (pg. 126)

Detailed Piping with Royal Icing
  (pg. 133)

## Materials

4⅛-inch (10.4 cm) frog cookie
  cutter

Run sugar icing: white, black,
  gray, light yellow, orange,
  brown, flesh

Royal icing, soft peak: white,
  black

Tip #1

1. Roll out the cookie dough and cut the frog shape. Cut off the legs of the frog to create a hamster body. Bake and cool the cookies.

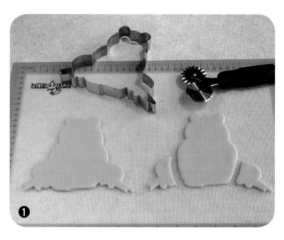

2. If the hamster has white on his head and belly, outline and fill the white part first using white run sugar. Outline and fill the body and head with the desired color of run sugar icing, leaving space for his feet.

3. When the icing is firm, pipe the hamster's cheeks using white run sugar icing and his arms using the run sugar color you chose in the previous step. Pipe his hands and feet using flesh run sugar icing. Allow the cheeks to set. Pipe his nose using brown run sugar icing. Pipe his eyes using black run sugar icing.

4. Fit a pastry bag with tip #1. Fill the bag with black soft peak royal icing. Outline his eyes and nose, and pipe the mouth using black soft peak royal icing. Fit a pastry bag with tip #1. Fill the bag with white soft peak royal icing. Pipe his whiskers using white soft peak royal icing.

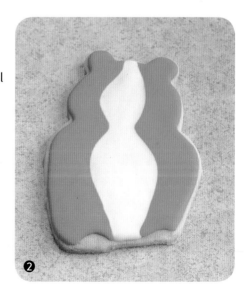

Birdcage Cookies

## Techniques

Trimming the Cut Cookie Dough (pg. 118)

Detailed Piping with Royal Icing (pg. 133)

Rolled Fondant (pg. 137)

## Materials

3⅜-inch (8.6 cm) bell cookie cutter

4-inch (10 cm) bell cookie cutter

4-inch (10 cm) acorn cookie cutter

¾-inch (2 cm) mini dove cookie cutter

Pizza cutter

Rolled fondant: white, pink, lime green, light blue, lavender

Royal icing, soft peak: black

Tip #1

Black nonpareils

Piping gel

1. Roll out the cookie dough and cut out the bells and acorn shapes. With the pizza cutter, cut off the clappers of the two bells and the stalk of the acorn. Trim the edges of the middle bell. Bake and cool the birdcage cookies.

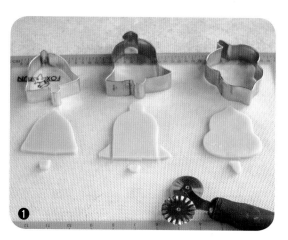

2. Knead and soften white rolled fondant. Roll the white fondant to 2 mm thickness. Cut the bell or acorn shape. Trim the clappers, stalk, or edge of the bell to match the baked cookie. Brush piping gel onto the baked and cooled cookies. Place the trimmed fondant shape on the cookie. Using the dove cutter, cut a dove from the birdcage. Knead and soften pink, green, lavender, or blue rolled fondant. Roll fondant to 2 mm thickness. Cut a dove. Replace the white dove shape you cut out with one of the colored doves. Add a black nonpareil for the bird's eye, using piping gel to attach.

3. Fit a pastry bag with tip #1. Fill the bag with black soft peak royal icing. Pipe the details onto the birdcage.

Kittens

## Techniques

Combine Cookie Dough Shapes
(pg. 118)

Run Sugar Icing (pg. 126)

Detailed Piping with Royal Icing
(pg. 133)

## Materials

5½-inch (14 cm) pup cookie
cutter

3⅝-inch (9.2 cm) kitten face
cookie cutter

Run sugar icing: white, black,
gray, orange, brown, ivory,
blue, pink

Royal icing, soft peak: black

Tip #1.5

1. Roll out the cookie dough and cut out the puppy shape and the kitten face. Cut off the head of the puppy shape using the kitten cutter. Place the kitten face over the dog body, slightly overlapping the dough. Gently press to blend the two cookies together. Bake and cool the kitten cookies.

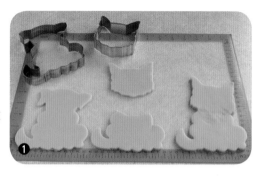

   When cool, turn the cookie over. Add royal icing to secure the seam where the head and body are connected.

2. If the kitten has a contrasting color on his face, feet, and belly, outline and fill that area first using run sugar. Outline and fill the kitten's body and head with the desired color of run sugar icing. Allow the kitten to set completely. When the icing is firm, pipe the kitten's nose and the inside of the ears using pink run sugar icing.

3. Pipe the kitten eyes with white run sugar icing. Immediately pipe a smaller dot inside the white eye using blue run sugar icing. Immediately pipe a smaller dot inside the blue area using black run sugar icing. Allow the eyes to set.

4. Fit a pastry bag with tip #1.5. Fill the bag with black soft peak royal icing and outline the kitten's body, ears, eyes, and nose. Pipe his whiskers.

Pretty Poodles

## Techniques

Rolled Fondant (pg. 137)

Detailed Piping with Royal Icing
  (pg. 133)

## Materials

5-inch (12.7 cm) poodle cookie
  cutter

Oval scalloped cookie cutters:
  25mm x 20mm and 30mm x
  25mm

Round scalloped cookie cutters:
  60mm and 25mm

Mini accent set: triangle cutter,
  19mm

Curly texture mat

Rolled fondant: white, black,
  pink, light pink, gray, light gray

Royal icing, soft peak: black

Tip #1

Piping gel

1. Roll out the cookie dough and cut out the poodle
   shape. Bake and cool the poodle cookies. Brush
   piping gel on the baked and cooled cookies.

2. Knead and soften pink rolled fondant. Roll to 2
   mm. With the same cutter used in baking, cut out
   the poodle shape. Lift the shape and place on the
   cookie brushed with piping gel. Fit a pastry bag
   with tip #1. Fill the bag with black soft peak royal
   icing. Outline the poodle.

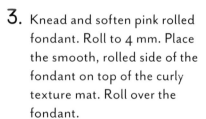

3. Knead and soften pink rolled
   fondant. Roll to 4 mm. Place
   the smooth, rolled side of the
   fondant on top of the curly
   texture mat. Roll over the
   fondant.

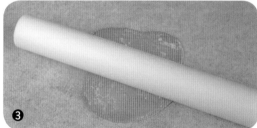

4. Flip the mat over and onto the work
   surface. Peel back the mat. Cut three 25 x
   20 mm ovals. Cut one 30 x 25 mm oval.
   Cut one 25 mm scalloped round. Cut one
   60mm round. Place the ovals and circles on
   the poodle using piping gel to attach.

5. Fit a pastry bag with tip #1. Fill the bag with
   black soft peak royal icing. Outline the
   scalloped pieces. Knead and soften light
   pink rolled fondant. Roll thin. Cut two small
   triangles for the bow. Attach to the poodle
   with piping gel.

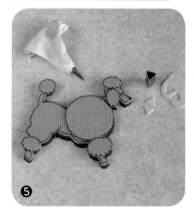

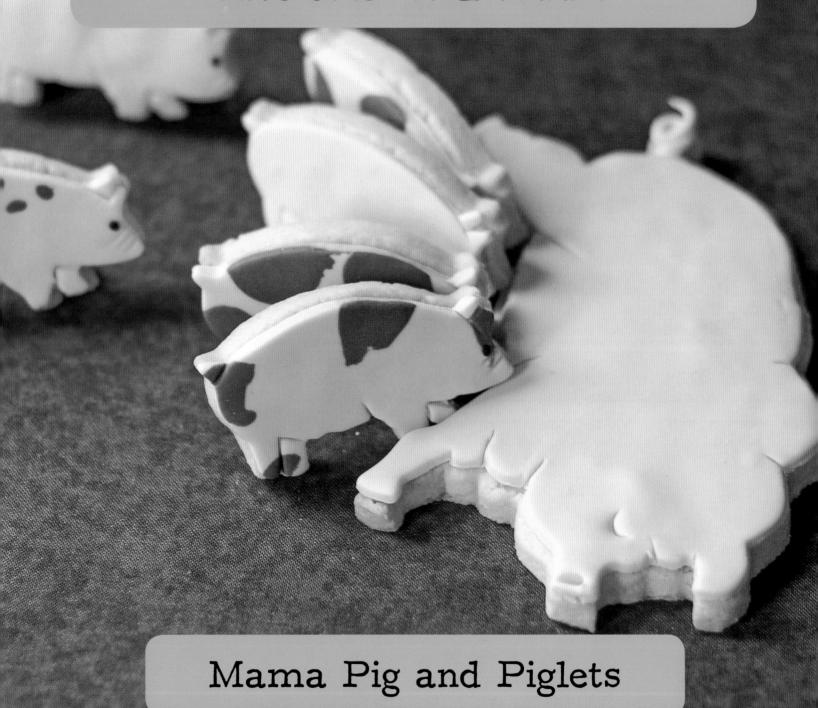

Mama Pig and Piglets

Rolled Fondant (pg. 137)

Embossing Rolled Fondant
   (pg.139)

## Materials

5½-inch (14 cm) pig cookie cutter

1½-inch (3.8 cm) pig cookie
   cutter

Paring knife

Rolled fondant: light pink, dark
   gray, dark brown

Tip #10

Piping gel

Toothpick

# Mama Pig

1. Bake and cool the mama pig cookies. Knead and soften pink rolled fondant. Roll pink fondant to 2 mm thickness. Cut the pink rolled fondant using the mama pig cutter used in baking. Remove the tail using a paring knife. Brush the baked cookie with piping gel. Place the rolled fondant pig on the brushed cookie. Add lines using the dull side of the paring knife. Emboss the eye using tip #10. Emboss the nostril using a toothpick. Roll a small snake for the tail. Curl around a toothpick. Carefully remove the curled tail and attach to the cookie with piping gel.

# Piglets

2. Bake and cool the piglet cookies. Knead and soften pink rolled fondant. Roll pink fondant to 2 mm thickness. Knead and soften dark gray rolled fondant. Place small pieces of gray on top of the rolled pink fondant. Roll over the pink and gray to achieve spotted fondant.

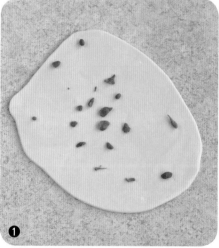

3. Cut the spotted rolled fondant using the small pig cutter used in baking. Brush the baked cookie with piping gel. Place the rolled fondant pig on the brushed cookie. Add lines using the dull side of the paring knife. Roll a tiny ball for the eye using dark brown rolled fondant and attach with piping gel.

Rooster and Chicks

## Materials

4-inch (10 cm) rooster cookie
cutter

2½-inch (6.4 cm) chick cookie
cutter

Run sugar icing: white, orange,
red, yellow

Royal icing, soft peak: black

Tip #1.5

Sanding sugar: yellow

# Rooster

1. Stretch the rooster cutter to give the rooster a whimsical shape. Cut, bake, and cool the rooster cookies. Outline and fill the rooster shape using white run sugar icing. Allow the icing to set completely. When the icing is firm, fit a pastry bag with tip #1.5. Fill the bag with black soft peak royal icing. Outline the rooster's body and wing, and pipe two dots for the eyes using the black soft peak royal icing. Pipe the rooster's comb using red run sugar icing. Pipe the rooster's legs and beak using orange run sugar icing.

# Chicks

2. Stretch the chick cutter to give the chick a whimsical shape. Bake and cool the chick cookies. Outline and fill the chick's body using yellow run sugar icing. Immediately sprinkle with yellow sanding sugar. Allow the icing to set completely. Pipe the chick's comb using yellow run sugar icing. Fit a pastry bag with tip #1.5. Fill the bag with black soft peak royal icing. Outline the chick's body and wing, and pipe two dots for the eyes using the black soft peak royal icing. Pipe the chick's legs and beak using orange run sugar icing.

Pastel Cows

## Techniques

Run Sugar Icing (pg. 126)

## Materials

4⅛-inch (10.4 cm) cow cookie cutter

Run sugar icing: white, black, ivory, light sky blue, sky blue, light pink, pink, light orange, orange, light electric green, electric green

1. Bake and cool the cow cookies. Outline and fill the cow's ears, body, front leg, and back leg with run sugar icing in the desired color. Immediately pipe on a contrasting color for the cow's spots. Allow to set completely.

2. When the icing is firm, pipe the cow's face and the remaining legs. Immediately pipe on a contrasting color for the cow's spot on his face. Allow to set completely. When the icing is firm, pipe the cow's nose and horns with ivory run sugar icing. Using black run sugar icing, pipe his eyes and nostrils.

Down the Bunny Hole

## Techniques

Trimming the Cut Cookie Dough (pg. 118)

Run Sugar Icing (pg. 126)

Detailed Piping with Royal Icing (pg. 133)

Buttercream Icing (pg. 136)

## Materials

6-inch (15 cm) bunny cookie cutter (side view bunny)

5½-inch (14 cm) bunny cookie cutter (front view bunny)

5½-inch (14 cm) teddy bear cookie cutter (bunny legs)

2-inch (5 cm) carrot cookie cutter

3½-inch (9 cm) fluted round cookie cutter

Mini pizza cutter

Run sugar icing: white, pink, orange, light orange, green

Royal icing, soft peak: white, black

Buttercream icing: light green, chocolate

Tips #1.5, #1, #2A, and #233

Fine chocolate cookie crumbs

# Bunny Head, Legs, and Carrot

1. Roll out the cookie dough. Cut the side view bunny, the front view bunny, teddy bear, carrot, and bunny hole. Cut apart the body and head of the bunnies, using a mini pizza cutter. Cut off the legs of the bear. Reuse and reroll the dough left from the bunny body and the teddy bear upper body. Bake and cool the cookies.

2. Outline and fill the heads and legs using white run sugar icing. Immediately pipe pink inside the ears of the front-facing bunny and on the paws of the bunny legs. Allow the icing to set completely.

3. Outline the bunny using white royal icing and tip #1.5. Pipe the whiskers, eyes, and mouth using black royal icing and tip #1. Pipe a nose with pink run sugar icing. Allow all the iced cookies to set for one day.

4. Outline and fill the carrot using orange run sugar icing. Immediately pipe dots on the carrot using light orange run sugar icing. Outline and fill the carrot tops using green run sugar icing.

5. Using chocolate buttercream icing and tip #2A, pipe a 2-inch (5 cm) circle in the center of the baked bunny hole cookie. Immediately sprinkle the circle with fine chocolate cookie crumbs. Pipe grass around the chocolate circle using tip #233 and light green buttercream icing. Place the hardened bunny faces and legs into the 2-inch (5 cm) chocolate circles.

Hobbyhorses

## Techniques

Cookies on a Stick (pg. 117)

Rolled Fondant (pg. 137)

Edible Frosting Sheets (pg. 143)

## Materials

4½-inch (11.4 cm) horse head cookie cutter

Strip cookie cutter: 7 mm

Oval cookie cutter: 8 x 10 mm

Round cookie cutters: 8 mm and 10 mm

Paring knife

Rolled fondant: white, black, dark brown, pink, lime green, turquoise, light orange

Edible frosting sheets: Vintage Tea

Cookie sticks

Fondant extruder

Piping gel

Toothpick

Straws (optional)

1. Bake the horse head cookies on a stick and allow them to cool. Roll enough white rolled fondant to fit the frosting sheet, rolling to 2 mm thickness. Remove the frosting sheet from the paper backing. Turn over the frosting sheet. Brush the back of the frosting sheet with a thin layer of piping gel. Place the frosting sheet on the rolled fondant. Gently roll over the fondant with minimal pressure to completely attach.

2. Brush the baked and cooled cookies with piping gel. With the same cutter used in baking, cut the patterned fondant. Gently lift the cut shapes and place on the piping gel-coated cookies. Take care when lifting the pieces, as the frosting sheet may wrinkle. Cut the fondant off of the mane of the horse.

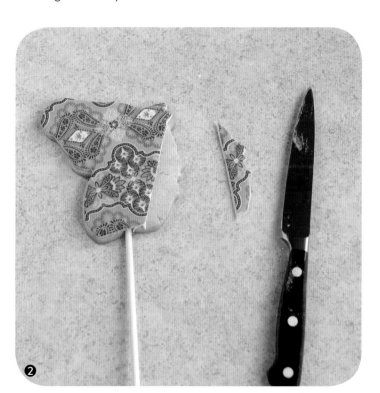

(CONTINUED)

These horse heads resemble hand-sewn hobbyhorses. The horse manes are thick with rolled fondant, so be sure to MAKE THE BAKED COOKIES THICKER THAN USUAL.

**3.** Knead and soften brown rolled fondant. Roll thin. Gently press a strip cutter into the brown fondant.

**5.** Knead and soften rolled fondant in the desired color for the horse's mane. Fit an extruder with the clover disk. Feed the extruder with softened fondant. Extrude the fondant. Twist to create a braided effect. Cut pieces and attach to the horse with piping gel.

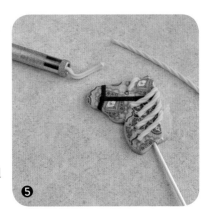

**4.** Use the strip cutter to cut the horse's bridle. Place on the horse head, using piping gel to attach.

**6.** Knead and soften brown rolled fondant. Roll thin. Cut the nostril using a mini oval cutter. Knead and soften black rolled fondant. Roll thin. Cut the eye using a small round cutter. Emboss the eye using a smaller round cutter. Create holes in the eye using a toothpick to resemble a button. Place the features on the horse, using piping gel to attach. After the cookies are decorated, insert the sticks into decorative straws.

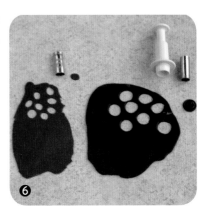

# IN NATURE

## Woodland Friends

## Techniques

Trimming the Cut Cookie Dough (pg. 118)

Layer Baked Shapes (pg. 118)

Run Sugar Icing (pg. 126)

Detailed Piping with Royal Icing (pg. 133)

## Materials

4-inch (10 cm) skunk cookie cutter

3-inch (7.5 cm) squirrel cookie cutter

4-inch (10 cm) cat cookie cutter (fox and raccoon)

Run sugar icing: white, black, pink, brown, ivory, dark ivory, gray, dark gray, terra-cotta

Royal icing, soft peak: chocolate brown

Tip #1.5

## Skunk

1. Bake and cool the skunk cookies. Outline and fill the white streak on the head, back, and tail using white run sugar icing. Outline the body, tail, front leg, and back leg with black run sugar icing. Allow the white and black icing to set completely.

2. When the icing is firm, pipe the skunk's ears with black run sugar icing. Pipe a nose with pink run sugar icing. Pipe the eye with brown run sugar icing.

## Squirrel

1. Bake and cool the squirrel cookies. Outline and fill the belly and eye detail using ivory run sugar icing. Outline the body with dark ivory run sugar icing. Allow the ivory and dark ivory icing to set completely.

2. When the icing is firm, pipe the squirrel's ears, leg, tail, and arm with dark ivory run sugar icing. Pipe an eye and the nose with black run sugar icing.

# Raccoon

1. Bake and cool the raccoon cookies. Outline and fill the belly using gray run sugar icing. Outline and fill the body with dark gray run sugar icing. Allow the icing to set completely.

2. When the icing is firm, pipe the raccoon's tail stripes using gray and dark gray run sugar icing. Pipe the arms using dark gray run sugar icing. Pipe the raccoon's mask with dark gray icing. Pipe the rest of the raccoon's face using gray icing, taking care around the mask. Allow the icing to set completely.

3. Pipe the eyes and the nose with black run sugar icing.

# Fox

1. Bake and cool the fox cookies. Outline and fill the belly using ivory run sugar icing. Outline and fill the body with terra-cotta run sugar icing. Allow the icing to set completely.

2. When the icing is firm, pipe the fox's tail using ivory and terra-cotta run sugar icing. Pipe the arms using terra-cotta run sugar icing. Pipe the fox's cheeks with ivory icing. Pipe the rest of the fox's face using terra-cotta icing, taking care around the cheeks. Allow the icing to set completely.

3. Pipe the eyes and the nose with black run sugar icing.

# Fox in Log

1. Roll out the cookie dough. Cut out the fox cookie, trimming around his face before baking. Remove the body. Cut 3¼ x 2½ inch (9.5 x 6.4 cm) rectangular logs with one jagged end. Bake and cool the fox face and log cookies.

2. Pipe the fox's cheeks with ivory icing. Pipe the rest of the fox's face using terra-cotta icing, taking care around the cheeks. Allow the icing to set completely. Pipe the eyes and the nose with black run sugar icing.

3. Outline and fill a circle in the middle of the log using black run sugar icing. Outline and fill the remainder of the log with chocolate brown run sugar icing. Allow the icing to set completely.

4. When the icing is firm, fit a pastry bag with tip #1.5. Fill the bag with chocolate brown soft peak royal icing. Pipe the log details using chocolate brown soft peak royal icing. Attach the fox face with chocolate brown royal icing.

Turtle Stack

## Techniques

Combine Cookie Dough Shapes (pg. 118)

Run Sugar Icing (pg. 126)

Detailed Piping with Royal Icing (pg. 133)

## Materials

5¾-inch (14.6 cm) turtle cookie cutter

5-inch (12.7 cm) turtle cookie cutter

3¼-inch (8.3 cm) turtle cookie cutter

Run sugar icing: light pink, deep pink, light gold, gold, light avocado, avocado, red, turquoise, copper

Royal icing, soft peak: chocolate brown

Tip #1.5

# Baking Instructions

1. Cut out the large, medium, and small turtles. Place the large turtle on a silicone or parchment-lined baking sheet. Place the medium turtle on top of the large turtle, overlapping the feet onto the shell by approximately ¼ inch (6 mm). Place the small turtle on the top of the medium turtle, overlapping the legs onto the shell by approximately ¼ inch (6 mm). Gently press to blend the cookies. Bake and cool the stacked turtle cookie. When cool, turn the cookie over. Add royal icing to secure the seams where the turtles are connected.

# Small Turtle

2. Outline and fill the shell using light pink run sugar icing. Immediately pipe dots with all the other colors of run sugar. Outline and fill the legs and face with deep pink run sugar. Allow the icing to set completely.

# Medium Turtle

3. Outline and fill the shell using light gold run sugar icing. Immediately pipe stripes with all the other colors of run sugar. Outline and fill the legs and face with gold run sugar. Allow the icing to set completely.

# Large Turtle

4. Outline and fill the shell using light avocado run sugar icing. Immediately pipe dots with all the other colors of run sugar. Outline and fill the legs and face with avocado run sugar. Allow the icing to set completely.

5. When the icing is firm, outline the turtles and pipe the eyes and mouths using chocolate brown soft peak royal icing and tip #1.5.

Snails

## Techniques

Rolled Fondant (pg. 137)

Embossing Rolled Fondant
(pg. 139)

## Materials

2¾-inch (7 cm) snail cookie
cutter

Flower plunger cutter

Rolled fondant: light green,
green, light orange, orange,
light pink, pink

Tip #10

Black nonpareils

Piping gel

1. Bake and cool the snail cookies. Knead and soften light green rolled fondant. Roll the fondant into a long snake that is tapered at one end. Knead and soften green rolled fondant. Roll the fondant into a short snake that is tapered at one end. Roll light orange fondant thin. Cut a small flower using the flower plunger cutter, or if the snail has spots, roll several small balls.

2. Roll a small ball using orange fondant. Attach it to the center of the flower with piping gel. Slightly flatten the snakes with the palms of your hands. Brush the baked cookie with piping gel. Curl the long snake and place on the brushed cookie for the shell. Place the short snake on the brushed cookie for the snail's body.

3. Emboss the mouth using tip #10. Attach black nonpareils with piping gel for the eyes. Roll two thin snakes for the antennae and attach with piping gel. Note: If the snail has spots instead of a flower, roll a few small balls of a contrasting color, then flatten. Attach to the snail with piping gel.

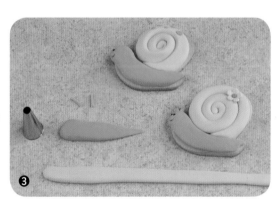

Chubby Frogs

## Techniques

Trimming the Cut Cookie Dough (pg. 118)

Combine Cookie Dough Shapes (pg. 118)

Run Sugar Icing (pg. 126)

Detailed Piping with Royal Icing (pg. 133)

## Materials

3-inch (7.5 cm) bear head cookie cutter

3 ¼-inch (8.3 cm) frog cookie cutter

Run sugar icing: white, black, light green, green, pink, yellow

Royal icing, soft peak: chocolate brown

Tip #1

1. Roll out the cookie dough. Cut out one bear head and one frog. Cut the legs off the frog. Place the legs on the sides of the bear head with a slight overlap, creating a chubby frog. Gently press to combine shapes. Bake and cool the frog cookies. When cool, turn the cookie over. Add royal icing to secure the seam where the body and legs are connected.

2. Outline and fill the belly using light green run sugar icing. Outline and fill the body with green run sugar icing, leaving space for the whites of the eyes. Immediately pipe two pink circles for the frog's cheeks. Outline and fill the eyes with white run sugar. Allow the icing to set completely. When the icing is firm, pipe the frog's pupils using black run sugar icing. Pipe the legs using green run sugar icing. Pipe dots using yellow run sugar icing.

3. Fit a pastry bag with tip #1. Fill the bag with chocolate brown soft peak royal icing. Pipe the mouth using chocolate brown soft peak royal icing.

Fluttering Friends

## Techniques

Rolled Fondant (pg. 137)

Edible Frosting Sheets (pg. 143)

## Materials

Cutie cupcake cutters: Fluttering Friends

Edible frosting sheets: Fluttering Friends

Rolled fondant: white

Piping gel

1. Bake and cool the fluttering friends cookies. Roll enough white rolled fondant to fit the frosting sheets, rolling to 2 mm thickness. Remove the frosting sheet from the paper backing. Turn over the frosting sheet and brush the back with a thin layer of piping gel.

2. Place the frosting sheet on the rolled fondant. Gently roll over the fondant with minimal pressure to completely attach. Brush the baked and cooled cookies with piping gel. Line up the cutter with the patterned rolled fondant. Cut out the patterned rolled fondant. Gently lift the cut shapes and place on the corresponding piping gel-coated cookies.

Bird Family

## Techniques

Trimming the Cut Cookie Dough
(pg. 118)

Run Sugar Icing (pg. 126)

Detailed Piping with Royal Icing
(pg. 133)

## Materials

5-inch (12.7 cm) lovebird cookie
cutter

5⅛-inch (13 cm) banana split
cookie cutter

Run sugar icing: light blue, blue,
yellow, pink, light pink, light
green, green, orange, chocolate
brown

Royal icing, soft peak: chocolate
brown

Tips #0 and #1.5

# Mama and Daddy Birds

1.  Bake and cool the bird cookies (make half
facing in one direction and half facing in the
other direction). Outline and fill the daddy
bird shape using light blue run sugar icing,
leaving space for the belly. Immediately
pipe the belly using yellow run sugar icing.
Outline and fill the mama bird shape using
light pink run sugar icing, leaving space for
the belly. Immediately pipe the belly using
light green run sugar icing. Allow the icing to
set completely.

2.  When the icing is firm, outline and fill the wing of the daddy bird with blue
run sugar icing. Outline and fill the wing of the mama bird with pink run sugar
icing. Pipe the beaks and feet of both birds using orange run sugar icing. Fit a
pastry bag with tip #0. Fill the bag with brown soft peak royal icing. Pipe the
eyelashes and eyebrows using brown royal icing. Pipe a dot for the eye using
brown run sugar icing.

# Baby Birds

3.  Roll out the cookie dough. Cut out the
banana split shape. Cut the base off the
bowl. Bake and cool the nest cookie.

4.  Outline and fill the nest using brown
run sugar icing. Outline and fill the
left bird using blue run sugar icing,
leaving space for the belly. Pipe the
belly using light blue run sugar icing.
Outline and fill the center bird using
yellow run sugar icing. Outline and

fill the right bird using green run sugar icing, leaving space for the belly. Pipe
the belly using light green run sugar icing. Allow the icing to set completely.
Use orange run sugar icing to pipe the beaks. Pipe the eyes using black run
sugar icing. Fit a pastry bag with tip #1.5. Fill the bag with brown soft peak
royal icing. Pipe overlapping twigs for the nest.

Owls

Run Sugar Icing (pg. 126)

Rolled Fondant (pg. 137)

Embossing Rolled Fondant (pg. 139)

## Materials

Dottie frame cookie cutter set

Cutie cupcake cutter set: owl cookie cutter

Mini accent cookie cutter set: football cutter for wings and round cutter for eyes

Plunger cutter set: round

Paring knife

Run sugar icing: gray, white

Rolled fondant: light blue, white, light green, dark gray, golden yellow, orange

Tip #10

Piping gel

1. Bake and cool the plaque cookies. Outline and fill the plaque shape using gray run sugar icing. Immediately pipe the dots using white run sugar icing. Set aside for several hours or overnight, allowing the icing to set completely.

2. Knead and soften light blue rolled fondant. Roll thin. Cut out the owl. Immediately emboss the feathers on the bottom half of the owl using the small football cutter. Knead and soften white rolled fondant. Roll thin. Cut the eyes using the round cutter. Knead and soften light green rolled fondant. Roll thin. Cut the eyes using a round plunger cutter. Knead and soften dark gray rolled fondant. Roll thin. Cut the eyes using tip #10. Knead and soften golden yellow rolled fondant. Roll thin. Cut the wings using the large football cutter. Knead and soften orange rolled fondant. Roll thin. Cut the beak using a paring knife.

3. Place the owls on the plaque cookies using piping gel to attach. Attach the owl's features with piping gel.

Hedgehogs

## Techniques

Trimming the Cut Cookie Dough
  (pg. 118)

Run Sugar Icing (pg. 126)

Painted Cookies (pg. 134)

## Materials

5-inch (12.7 cm) flower cookie
  cutter

4¼-inch (10.8 cm) hedgehog
  cookie cutter

2½-inch (6.4 cm) leaf cookie
  cutter

Run sugar icing: white

Food color: ivory, blue, yellow,
  green, brown, black

1. Roll out the cookie dough. Cut out the flower. Cut the top petals off the flower, rounding the center. Cut out the hedgehog and leaf cookies. Bake and cool the cookies.

2. Ice the cookies with white run sugar icing. Allow the cookies to crust for 24 hours before painting.

❶

3. Fill each cavity of a paint tray half full with water. Squirt small amounts of food color gel onto the top of the paint tray. Blend some of the food color gel with the water in the cavities to achieve a soft shade. Test the color on a white sheet of paper. Outline the hedgehog details with a very light shade of ivory. Outline the flower petals with a very light shade of blue. Outline the center of the flower with a light shade of yellow. Outline the leaves with a light shade of green. Paint the hedgehog, flower, and leaves using very light shades of the desired colors. Leave a thin white line in between adjoining colors to keep them from bleeding into one another. Blend the concentrated food color on the top of the paint tray with a small amount of water to create a thick, darker color for shading. Test the color on a white sheet of paper. Use the shading color to add contrast and shading to the cookie. Allow the painted cookie to dry for several hours. Outline the cookie using a fine brush with concentrated black food color.

Gilded Butterflies

## Techniques
Rolled Fondant (pg. 137)

## Materials
Butterfly cookie cutter texture set

Rolled fondant: two or three shades of blue, two or three shades of purple, two or three shades of green

Piping gel

Gold dusting powder

Grain alcohol

Brush

1. Bake and cool the cookies. Roll the fondants to 4 mm thickness. Set the butterfly texture mat, raised side down. Place the smooth, rolled side of the fondant on top of the butterfly texture mat. Roll over the fondant.

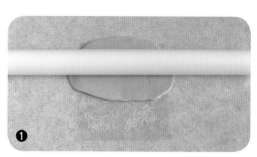

2. Flip the mat over and peel back the mat.

3. Brush piping gel onto the cookies. Line up the cookie cutter used in baking with the embossed design. Cut the butterfly. Place the textured butterfly on the cookie.

4. Create a paint using gold dusting powder mixed with grain alcohol. Paint the raised, textured butterfly. Holding the brush as parallel to the work surface as possible is best, as the bristles will only touch the raised areas.

EITHER SIDE of the texture mat may be used. Using the side of the mat that gives a raised impression will make it easy to paint.

Lacey Lovebirds

## Techniques

Rolled Fondant (pg. 137)

Detailed Piping with Royal Icing
  (pg. 133)

## Materials

4½-inch (11.4 cm) bird cookie
  cutter

Rolled fondant: white, pink,
  peach, yellow, light green, sky
  blue, lavender

Royal icing, soft peak: white

Tips #1 and #8

Piping gel

Eyelet cutters

Needle scriber tool

Ball tool

1. Bake and cool the bird
   cookies. Brush piping gel onto
   the cookies. Knead and soften
   white rolled fondant. Roll to
   2 mm thickness. Knead and
   soften pink (or desired color)
   rolled fondant. Roll to 2 mm
   thickness. Place the white
   fondant on top of the pink

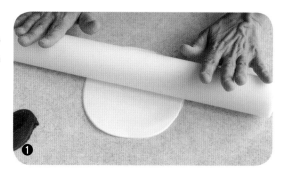

   fondant. Gently and evenly roll over the fondant to adhere to one another.
   Test to see if the rolled fondant layers are sticking together. If not, brush a
   small amount of water on top of the bottom layer.

2. With the same cutter used in
   baking, cut the fondant. Place the
   layered fondant on the cookie.
   Press an eyelet cutter into the
   rolled fondant-covered cookie.
   The cutter should cut completely
   through the first layer, but not the
   second layer. Do not press too
   firmly or the cookie will break.

(CONTINUED)

**3.** Lift the eyelet cutter and remove the cut pieces of the top rolled fondant layer using a toothpick or a needle scriber tool. If the cookie is showing through the cut shape, the cutter was pressed into the second layer of fondant.

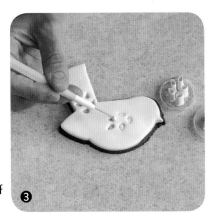

**5.** Tip #8 can be used in place of or in addition to an eyelet cutter to create round openings.

**4.** Press a ball tool into the cut designs to soften the cutouts and blend the top layer with the bottom.

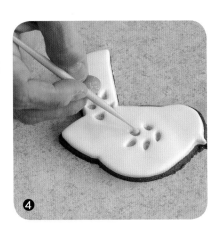

**6.** Fit a pastry bag with tip #1. Fill the bag with white soft peak royal icing. Pipe around the cutouts and pipe dots.

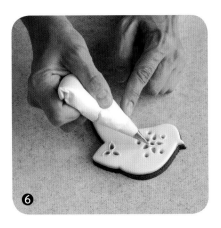

Rats

## Techniques

Make Cardstock Patterns
   (pg. 119)

Rolled Fondant (pg. 137)

Edible Frosting Sheets (pg. 143)

Detailed Piping with Royal Icing
   (pg. 133)

## Materials

6-inch (15 cm) standing rat
   cookie cutter

6-inch (15 cm) creeping rat
   cookie cutter

Mini pizza cutter

Cardstock, 4 x 6 inches (10 x
   15.2 cm)

Cardstock, 3 x 7 inches (7.6 x
   17.5 cm)

Rolled fondant: white, black

Edible frosting sheets

Royal icing, soft peak: black

Tip #1.5

Piping gel

1. Roll out the cookie dough. Lightly spray the cardstock rectangles with cooking spray. Place the cardstock on the cookie dough, sprayed side down. Use a pizza cutter to cut the rectangles. Bake and cool the rectangles.

2. Roll enough white rolled fondant to fit the rectangles, rolling to 2 mm thickness. Remove the frosting sheet from the paper backing. Turn over the frosting sheet and brush the back with a thin layer of piping gel. Place the frosting sheet on the rolled fondant. Gently roll over the fondant with minimal pressure to completely attach. Use the same pattern you used to cut the cookies and trim the edible frosting sheet.

3. Brush the baked and cooled rectangle cookies with piping gel. Place the printed fondant rectangle on the baked and cooled cookies.

4. Knead and soften black rolled fondant. Roll thin. Cut out the rats. Place the cut rats on the rectangle cookies, using piping gel to attach.

5. Fit a pastry bag with tip #1.5. Fill the bag with black soft peak royal icing. Outline the rectangle cookies.

Silly Spiders

## Techniques

Combine Cookie Dough Shapes (pg. 118)

Rolled Fondant (pg. 137)

Edible Frosting Sheets (pg. 143)

Detailed Piping with Royal Icing (pg. 133)

## Materials

1⅞-inch (4.8 cm) ladybug cookie cutter

1-inch (2.5 cm) square cookie cutter

1-inch (2.5 cm) round cookie cutter

4¼-inch (10.8 cm) spiderweb cookie cutter

Paring knife

Rolled fondant: white, lime green, red-orange, yellow, sky blue

Edible frosting sheets

Royal icing, soft peak: red, yellow, blue, green

Tips #1A and #1.5

Fondant extruder

Piping gel

Icing eyes: ⅛-inch (3 mm) and ⅜-inch (1 cm)

1. Roll out the cookie dough. Cut one ladybug and two squares for each spider. Place the squares on each side of the ladybug, slightly overlapping the squares with the ladybug to create a spider shape. Bake and cool the spider cookies. When cool, turn the cookie over. Add royal icing to secure the seam where the legs and body are connected.

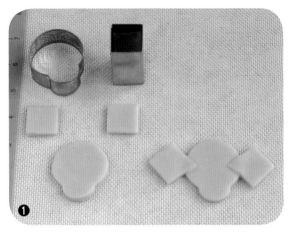

2. Roll enough white rolled fondant to fit the frosting sheet, rolling to 2 mm thickness. Remove the frosting sheet from the paper backing. Turn over the frosting sheet and brush the back with a thin layer of piping gel. Place the frosting sheet on the rolled fondant. Gently roll over the fondant with minimal pressure to completely attach.

3. Brush the baked and cooled spider cookies with piping gel. Cut the ladybug shape from the frosting sheet fondant. Gently lift the cut ladybug and place on the piping gel-coated cookies. Knead and soften the desired fondant color for the head. Cut a circle with a 1-inch (2.5 cm) round cutter. Emboss a mouth using tip #1A. Place the head on the spider body, using piping gel to attach.

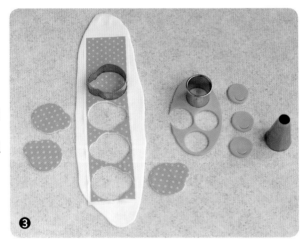

**4.** Knead and soften the fondant color used for the head and feed into the fondant extruder. Attach the disk with multiple openings. Extrude the fondant. Use a paring knife to cut the extruded fondant. Separate each strand. Brush piping gel onto the cookies where the spider's legs will be. Apply the legs. If the legs are too long, cut the excess using a paring knife. Attach the icing eyes, one of each size, with piping gel.

**5.** Bake and cool the spiderweb cookies. Knead and soften the white rolled fondant. Roll the white fondant to 2 mm thickness. Cut a spiderweb with the same cutter used in baking. Brush piping gel on the baked and cooled cookies. Place the fondant spiderweb on the cookie. Fit a pastry bag with tip #1.5. Fill the bag with colored soft peak royal icing. Pipe the web.

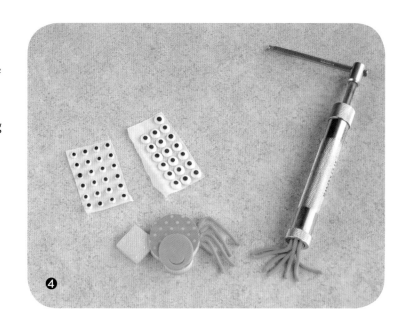

❹

Ladybugs & Bumblebees

## Materials

3-inch (7.5 cm) round cookie
cutter

2-inch (5 cm) heart cookie cutter

Paring knife

Run sugar icing: white, black,
red, yellow, pink

Royal icing: white

# Baking Instructions

1. Roll out the cookie dough. Cut
out two circles for the ladybug.
With a paring knife, cut one of
the circles in half for the ladybug's
wings. Cut one circle for the
bumblebee. Cut one heart for the
bumblebee's wings. Cut the heart
in half. Bake and cool the cookies.

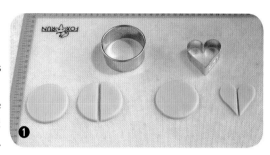

# Ladybug

2. Outline and fill the circle with
black run sugar icing. Outline
and fill the half circles with red
run sugar icing. Immediately
pipe dots with black run sugar
icing. Allow the icing to set
completely. When the icing is
firm, pipe the ladybug's eyes using black run sugar icing. Attach the wings to
the body using a small amount of royal icing.

# Bumblebee

3. Outline and fill the circle
with yellow run sugar icing.
Immediately pipe stripes with
black run sugar icing and
cheeks with pink run sugar
icing. Outline and fill the cut
hearts with white run sugar
icing. Allow the icing to set completely. When the icing is firm, pipe the
bumblebee's eyes using black run sugar icing. Attach the wings to the body
using a small amount of royal icing.

Bright Geckos

## Techniques

Run Sugar Icing (pg. 126)

Detailed Piping with Royal Icing (pg. 133)

Shading Iced Cookies (pg. 142)

## Materials

5¾-inch (14.6 cm) lizard cookie cutter

Run sugar icing: white

Dusting powder: red, orange, yellow, green, blue, purple

Royal icing, soft peak: black

Tip #1.5

Flat brush

1. Bake and cool the lizard cookies. Pipe the cookies with white run sugar icing. Allow the cookies to crust for 24 hours before dusting. Brush the dusting powder onto the hardened white icing.

2. Brush in a circular motion where the colors meet to blend the colors.

3. Fit a pastry bag with tip #1.5. Fill the bag with black soft peak royal icing. Outline the geckos. Pipe two dots for the eyes.

4. Hold the pastry bag at a 90-degree angle. Without squeezing the bag, gently tap the cookie to add tiny black dots.

Mice in Teacups

## Techniques

Trimming the Cut Cookie Dough (pg. 118)

Combine Cookie Dough Shapes (pg. 118)

Run Sugar Icing (pg. 126)

Painted Cookies (pg. 134)

## Materials

4-inch (10 cm) mouse cookie cutter

3½-inch (9 cm) teacup cookie cutter

Paring knife

Run sugar icing: white

Food color: black, pink, blue, flesh, yellow

Royal icing: white

Fine brush

1. Roll out the cookie dough. Cut one mouse and one teacup for each mouse in teacup cookie. Cut the mouse at the waist. Cut off the mouse hands. Place the mouse torso on the teacup, slightly overlapping the teacup and the mouse. Cut any additional mice cookies. Bake and cool the mouse cookies. When cool, turn the cookie over. Add royal icing to secure the seam where the mouse and teacup are connected.

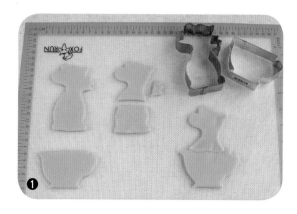

2. Ice the cookie with white run sugar icing. Allow the cookies to crust for 24 hours before painting. Fill each cavity of a paint tray half full with water. Squirt small amounts of food color gel onto the top of the paint tray. Blend some of the food color gel with the water in the cavities to achieve a soft shade. Test the color on a white sheet of paper. Outline the mouse details with a very light shade of gray. Outline the tail with a very light shade of pink. Outline the cup with a very light shade of desired color.

3. Paint the mouse and cup using very light shades. Leave a thin white line in between adjoining colors to keep the colors from bleeding into one another.

4. Blend the concentrated food color on the top of the paint tray with a small amount of water to create a thick, darker color for shading. Test the color on a white sheet of paper. Use the shading color to add contrast and shading to the cookie.

5. Allow the painted cookie to dry for several hours. Outline the cookie using a fine brush with concentrated food color.

Bats

## Techniques

Trimming the Cut Cookie Dough
(pg. 118)

Run Sugar Icing (pg. 126)

Detailed Piping with Royal Icing
(pg. 133)

## Materials

6¾ -inch (17 cm) bat cookie
cutter

Run sugar icing: ivory, brown,
and white

Royal icing, soft peak: dark
brown

Tips #8, #2, and #1

1. Roll out the cookie dough and cut the bat shape. Cut off the wings of some of the cookies to create a bat with folded wings. Using tip #8, cut a hole for hanging. Bake and cool the cookies.

2. Outline and fill the bat belly using ivory run sugar icing. Outline and fill the bat body and ears using brown run sugar icing. Allow the icing to set completely.

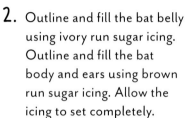

3. When the body and ears are set, pipe the head using ivory run sugar. Pipe the wings of the flying bat with ivory run sugar. Pipe one wing of the bat with the folded wings using brown run sugar icing. Allow the wings to harden. When the first wing is set on the bat folding his wings, pipe the other wing. Allow to harden.

4. Fit a pastry bag with tip #2. Fill the bag with brown soft peak royal icing. Outline the wings. Fit a pastry bag with tip #1. Fill the bag with brown soft peak royal icing. Pipe the mouth, nostrils, and eyes. Pipe the fangs with white run sugar icing.

Snakes

## Techniques

Trimming the Cut Cookie Dough (pg. 118)

Combine Cookie Dough Shapes (pg. 118)

Run Sugar Icing (pg. 126)

Detailed Piping with Royal Icing (pg. 133)

## Materials

4¼-inch (10.8 cm) coiled snake cookie cutter

5-inch (12.7 cm) slithering snake cookie cutter

2-inch (5 cm) oval cookie cutter

Paring knife

Run sugar icing: light orange, orange, teal, light yellow, yellow, green, red

Royal icing, soft peak: dark brown

Tip #1.5

1. Roll out the cookie dough and cut the coiled and slithering snakes. Cut an oval. Cut off the head of the slithering snake and replace with the oval. Bake and cool the cookies.

2. Outline and fill the nose using light orange run sugar icing. Outline and fill the head using teal run sugar icing. Immediately pipe on a triangle using orange run sugar icing. Pipe the neck and tail details using light orange run sugar icing, leaving spaces between sections. Outline and fill the bottom coil with teal run sugar icing. Immediately pipe triangles using orange run sugar icing. Allow the icing to set completely.

3. When set, pipe in between the neck and tail details using light orange run sugar icing, filling in the spaces. Outline and fill the top coil with teal run sugar icing. Immediately pipe triangles using orange run sugar icing. Allow the icing to set completely.

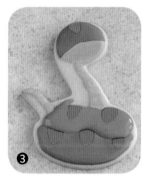

4. When the top coil is set, pipe the neck and the tail using teal run sugar icing. Immediately pipe triangles using orange run sugar icing. Fit a pastry bag with tip #1.5. Fill the bag with brown soft peak royal icing. Pipe the mouth, nostrils, and eyes.

5. Outline and fill the nose using light yellow run sugar icing. Outline and fill the snake body using green run sugar icing. Immediately pipe on the dots using yellow run sugar icing. Allow the icing to set completely. Fit a pastry bag with tip #1.Fill the bag with brown soft peak royal icing. Pipe the mouth, nostrils, and eyes.

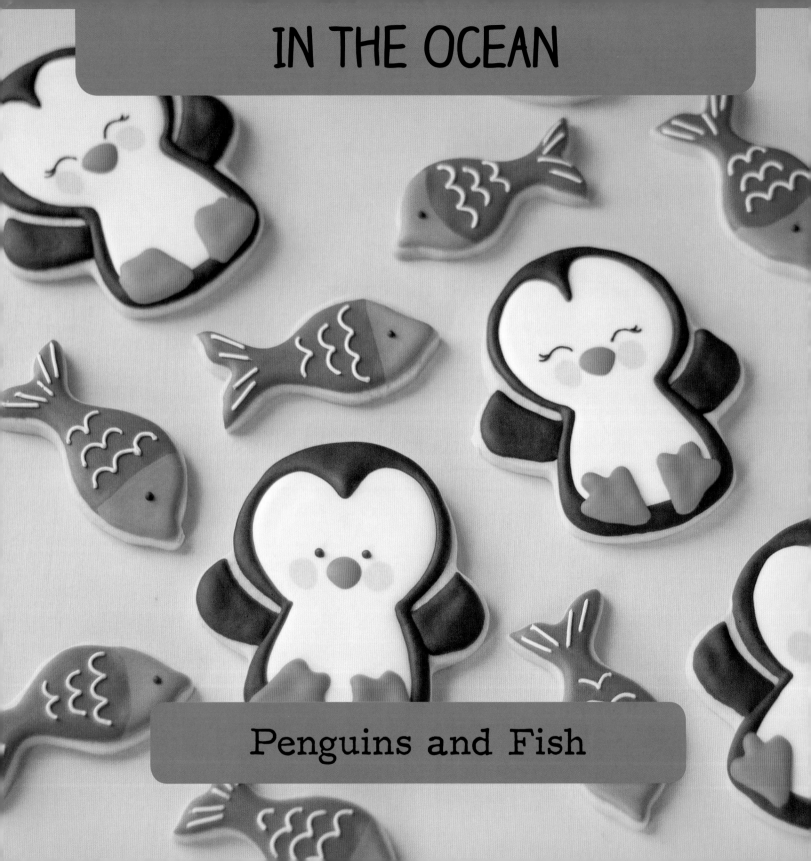

Penguins and Fish

## Techniques

Run Sugar Icing (pg. 126)

Detailed Piping with Royal Icing
(pg. 133)

## Materials

4-inch (10 cm) snowman head
cookie cutter used upside
down (for penguin body)

3-inch (7.5 cm) fish cookie cutter

Run sugar icing: white, pink,
black, orange, gray, navy blue

Royal icing, soft peak: black, light
blue

Tips #1 and #1.5

# Penguin

1. Bake and cool the penguin cookies.
   Outline and fill the penguin shape using
   white run sugar icing. Immediately pipe
   circles for the cheeks using pink run sugar
   icing. Allow the icing to set completely.

2. When the icing is firm, outline and fill the
   border and the head of the penguin with
   black run sugar icing. Allow the icing to
   set completely. When the black body is
   completely set, add the wings using black
   run sugar icing. Pipe the feet and the beak
   using orange run sugar icing. Fit a pastry bag
   with tip #1. Fill the bag with black soft peak
   royal icing and pipe the eyes.

# Fish

3. Bake and cool the fish cookies. Pipe the front third of the fish using gray run
   sugar icing. Immediately pipe the back two-thirds of the fish using navy run
   sugar icing. Allow the body to set completely. When the icing is firm, fit a
   pastry bag with tip #1.5. Fill the bag with light blue soft peak royal icing. Pipe
   the scales and fin details using light blue soft peak royal icing. Pipe the fish eye
   using black run sugar icing.

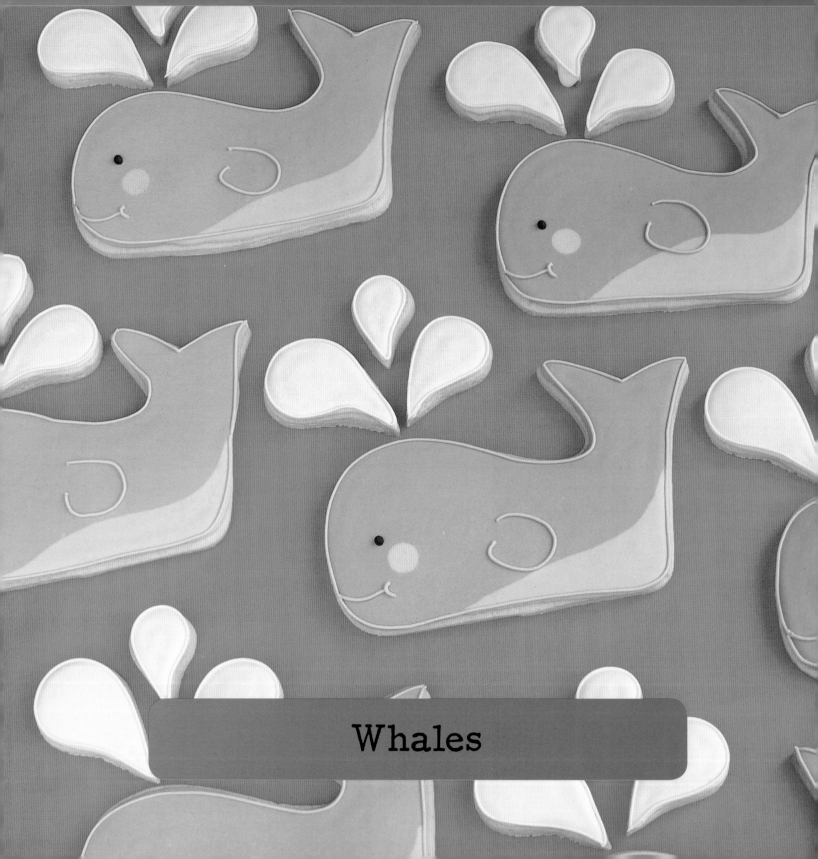

Whales

## Techniques

Run Sugar Icing (pg. 126)

Detailed Piping with Royal Icing
   (pg. 133)

## Materials

5¼- x 3 ¼-inch (13.3 x 8.3 cm)
   whale cookie cutter

1⅝-inch (4.1 cm) paisley cookie
   cutter

1¼-inch (3.2 cm) paisley cookie
   cutter

¾-inch (2 cm) paisley cookie
   cutter

Run sugar icing: white, light
   turquoise, turquoise, pink,
   brown

Royal icing, soft peak: turquoise,
   white

Tip #1.5

# Whale

1. Bake and cool the whale cookies. Outline and fill the whale belly using light turquoise run sugar icing. Outline and fill the rest of the whale using turquoise run sugar icing. Immediately pipe a dot for the cheek using pink run sugar icing. Allow the icing to set completely. When the icing is firm, fit a pastry bag with tip #1.5. Fill with turquoise soft peak royal icing. Outline the whale, add the mouth, and add the fin with turquoise soft peak icing. Pipe the eyes using brown run sugar icing.

# Whale Spout

2. Bake and cool the paisley cookies. Outline and fill the paisleys using white run sugar icing. Allow the icing to set completely. When the icing is firm, fit a pastry bag with tip #1.5. Fill with soft peak white royal icing. Outline the paisleys with white soft peak icing.

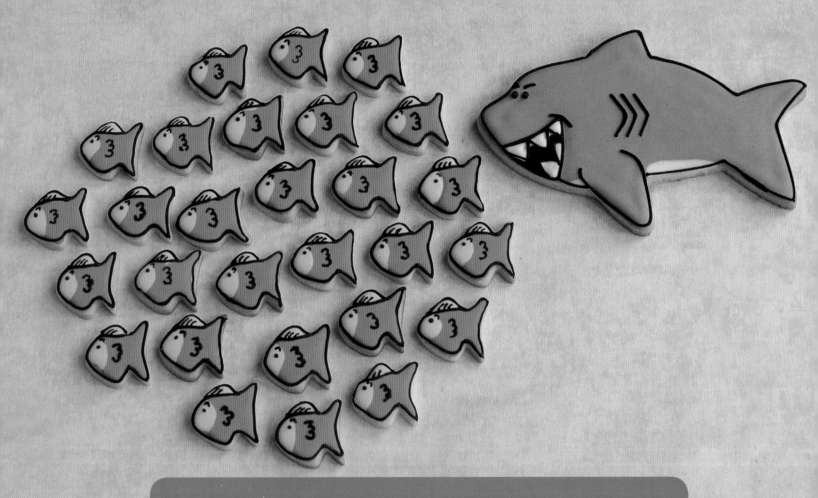

Shark and Fish

## Techniques

Run Sugar Icing (pg. 126)

Detailed Piping with Royal Icing
(pg. 133)

## Materials

5½-inch (14 cm) shark cookie
cutter

1-inch (2.5 cm) fish cookie cutter,

Run sugar icing: white, black,
blue, yellow, orange

Royal icing, soft peak: black

Tips #1.5 and #1

# Shark

1. Bake and cool the shark cookies. Outline and fill the shark belly using white run sugar icing. Outline and fill the shark's mouth using black run sugar icing. Outline and fill the shark body using blue run sugar icing. Allow the icing to set completely. When the icing is firm, pipe the teeth using white run sugar icing. Allow the icing to set completely. Fit a pastry bag with tip #1.5. Fill the bag with black soft peak royal icing. Pipe the outline and add details using black royal icing.

# Fish

2. Bake and cool the
fish cookies. Pipe the
front one-third of the
fish and top fin using
yellow run sugar icing.
Immediately pipe the
back two-thirds of the
fish using orange run
sugar icing. Allow the

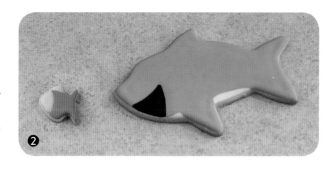

body to set completely. When the icing is firm, fit a pastry bag with tip #1. Fill the bag with black soft peak royal icing. Pipe the outline, fish eye, scales, and fin details using black soft peak royal icing.

Jumping Dolphins

## Techniques

Trimming the Cut Cookie Dough
(pg. 118)

Buttercream Icing (pg. 136)

Run Sugar Icing (pg. 126)

Detailed Piping with Royal Icing
(pg. 133)

## Materials

3¾-inch (9.5 cm) dolphin cookie
cutter

2¼-inch (5.7 cm) scalloped
round cookie cutter

Paring knife

Run sugar icing: gray, black

Royal icing, soft peak: gray

Buttercream icing: light blue

Tips #1.5 and #8

1. Roll out the cookie dough and cut the round cookies and dolphin shapes. With a paring knife, cut off the tail of the dolphin. Bake and cool the cookies.

2. Outline and fill the dolphin, except the dorsal fin, using gray run sugar icing. Allow the icing to set completely. When the icing is firm, pipe the dorsal fin using gray run sugar icing. Fit a pastry bag with tip #1.5. Fill the bag with gray soft peak royal icing. Pipe the outline of the flipper. Pipe the eye using black run sugar icing. Allow the dolphin to set overnight.

3. Fit a pastry bag with tip #8. Fill the bag with light blue buttercream. Pipe icing onto the cookie. Use a spatula to spread the icing smooth. Then hold the spatula directly above the iced cookie, press gently into the icing and lift quickly to create small peaks of icing.

4. Place the completely set dolphin cookie into the buttercream icing. Holding the bag at a 45-degree angle, insert the tip into the buttercream-iced cookie and squeeze the bag while lifting up, creating waves. Stop the pressure and pull away.

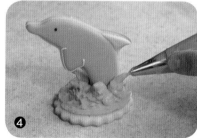

If the dolphin is not staying upright when placed on the round cookie, place a ball of fondant on the round cookie before spreading the buttercream icing. Spread the icing on the cookie and over the ball of fondant. Insert the dolphin into the ball of fondant and pipe waves.

Sea Creatures

## Techniques

Run Sugar Icing (pg. 126)

Detailed Piping with Royal Icing
  (pg. 133.)

## Materials

Octopus cookie cutter

Seahorse cookie cutter

Starfish cookie cutter

Fish cookie cutter

Run sugar icing: black, green,
  light green, blue, light blue,
  yellow, light yellow

Royal icing, soft peak: black

Tips #2 and #1.5

Tweezers

Black sugar pearls

1. Bake and cool the sea creature
   cookies. Fit a pastry bag with tip
   #2. Fill the bag with black run sugar
   icing. Outline the sea creatures
   using black run sugar icing. Allow
   the black outline to set.

2. When the black outline is set, fill pastry bags
   with colored run sugar icing. Fill in the details
   with the desired colors of run sugar icing. Use a
   toothpick to reach tight areas.

3. Immediately pipe dots with a contrasting color
   of run sugar icing.

4. Using tweezers, place the black sugar pearls for
   the eyes on the wet icing.

5. Fit a pastry bag with tip #1.5. Fill the bag
   with black soft peak royal icing. Pipe the sea
   creatures' mouths using black soft peak royal
   icing.

Polar Bears

## Techniques

Layer Baked Shapes (pg. 118)

Rolled Fondant (pg. 137)

## Materials

3-inch (7.5 cm) bear head cookie cutter

3⅞-inch (9.8 cm) snow globe cookie cutter

Paring knife

Ball tool

Ribbon cutter

Mini pizza cutter

Rolled fondant: white, black, red, sky blue

Royal icing: white

Tips #1A and #6

Piping gel

White sanding sugar

Black sugar pearls

1. Roll out the cookie dough. Cut one bear head and one snow globe for each polar bear. Bake and cool the polar bear cookies. Knead and soften white rolled fondant. Roll white fondant to 2 mm thickness. Cut the white rolled fondant using the bear cutter and snow globe cutter used in baking. Brush the baked cookie with piping gel. Place the rolled fondant pieces on the brushed cookie. Add lines for the mouth and legs using the dull side of the paring knife. Emboss the eyes and ears using a ball tool. Cut V-shaped eyelashes using a paring knife. Use tip #1A to emboss polar bear toes.

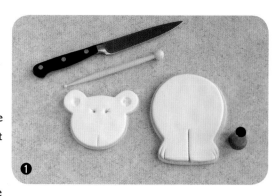

2. Brush a thin layer of piping gel onto the polar bear head and body. Sprinkle white sanding sugar on the tacky piping gel. Hold the cookie upside-down to allow the excess sugar to fall onto a parchment sheet.

(CONTINUED)

**3.** Add a dot of piping gel in the indented eyes and ears. Add sugar pearls for the eyes.

Knead and soften black rolled fondant. Roll two small balls for the ears. Insert the black balls into the indented ear and gently press to flatten. Roll one ball for the nose. Flatten and shape into a triangle. Add the nose, using piping gel to attach.

**4.** Knead and soften white rolled fondant. Roll thin. Use a ribbon cutter to cut even stripes. Repeat, making additional stripes with red and blue.

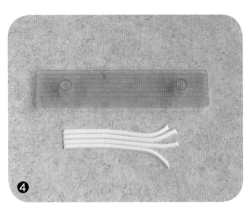

**5.** Place the cut stripes close to one another, nearly overlapping. Roll gently over the stripes to adhere them to one another. Cut the scarf shapes using a mini pizza cutter.

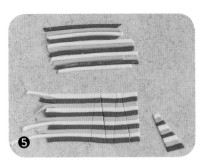

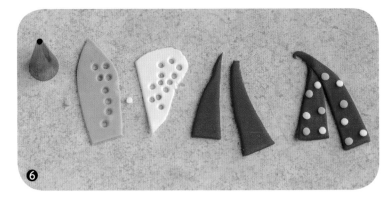

**6.** Knead and soften white rolled fondant. Roll thin. Cut small circles using tip #6. Repeat with blue rolled fondant. Knead and soften red rolled fondant. Cut the scarf shape. Add the cut circles to the scarf, using piping gel to attach.

**7.** Attach the polar bear head to the body using royal icing. Attach the scarf using piping gel.

Sock Monkeys

## Techniques

Rolled Fondant (pg. 137)

Painted Cookies (pg. 134)

## Materials

6¾ -inch (17.1 cm) sock monkey cookie cutter

Oval cookie cutter, 40 x 30 mm

Mini pizza cutter

Fabric texture mat set

Rolled fondant: white, red, and brown

Food color: brown, black

Fondant extruder

Brush

Piping gel

**1.** Bake and cool the monkey cookies. Brush piping gel onto the baked and cooled cookies. Knead and soften white rolled fondant. Roll to 4 mm thickness. Place the smooth, rolled side of the fondant on top of the knit mat from the fabric texture set. Roll over the fondant.

**2.** Flip the mat over and onto the work surface. Peel back the mat.

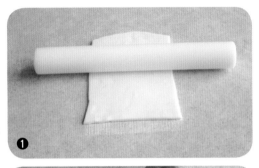

**3.** With the same cutter used in baking, cut the monkey. Cut the monkey into separate segments for the hat, ears, arms, hands, legs, and body. Set aside the hat, hands, and legs.

**4.** Arrange the body, arms, and ears on the piping gel-coated cookie. Add brown food color mixed with a small amount of black food color to a paint tray. Add a small amount of water to create a thin paint. Splatter the fondant-covered cookie by flicking the brush coated with the food color paint.

**5.** Arrange the hat, hands, and legs on the cookie, using piping gel to attach.

**6.** Knead and soften white rolled fondant. Roll thin. Cut an oval using the oval cutter for the mouth and chin area. Knead and soften red rolled fondant. Roll thin. Cut an oval using the oval cutter. Cut the oval in half for the mouth. Fit the fondant extruder with a disk with multiple round openings. Fill the extruder with kneaded and softened red rolled fondant. Extrude the fondant. Cut small pieces of the extruded fondant to create the tassel for the hat. Knead and soften brown rolled fondant. Roll two small balls for the eyes. Flatten the balls. Attach all the details with piping gel.

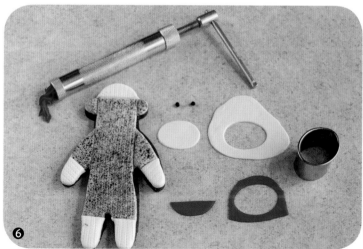

Cute Little Jungle Animals

## Techniques
Rolled Fondant (pg. 137)
Edible Frosting Sheets (pg. 143)

## Materials
Cutie cupcake cutters, Jungle

Edible frosting sheets, Jungle

Rolled fondant, white

Piping gel

1. Bake and cool the jungle animals.

2. Roll enough white rolled fondant to fit the jungle frosting sheets, rolling to 2 mm thickness. Remove frosting sheet from paper backing. Turn over the frosting sheet and brush the back of the frosting sheet with a thin layer of piping gel. Place the frosting sheet on the rolled fondant. Gently roll over the fondant with minimal pressure to completely attach.

3. Brush the baked and cooled animal cookies with piping gel. Line up the cutter with the patterned rolled fondant. Cut the patterned rolled fondant with the same cutters used in baking. Gently lift the cut shapes and place on piping gel-coated cookies.

Rainbow Bears

## Techniques
Run Sugar Icing (pg. 126)

## Materials
5½-inch (14 cm) teddy bear cookie cutter

Run sugar icing: red, peach, orange, egg yellow, lemon yellow, 1 part electric green plus 2 parts lemon yellow, electric green, leaf green, turquoise, electric blue, periwinkle, electric purple, fuchsia, deep pink, black, white

1. Bake and cool the bear cookies.

2. Outline and fill the belly and head using the desired run sugar icing color. Allow the icing to set completely.

3. When the icing is firm, outline and fill the cheeks, ears, arms, and legs. Allow the icing to set completely.

4. Pipe the nose and eyes using black run sugar icing. Add dots in the eyes using white run sugar icing.

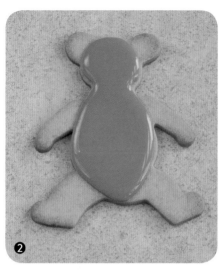

❷

❸

Flamingo Love

## Techniques

Detailed Piping with Royal Icing
  (pg. 133)

Run Sugar Icing (pg. 126)

## Materials

6-inch (15 cm) flamingo cookie
  cutter

2-inch (5 cm) heart cookie cutter

1-inch (2.5 cm) heart cookie
  cutter

Run sugar icing: black, pink, dark
  pink, light pink, golden yellow,
  and red

Royal icing, soft peak: pink

Tips: #1.5 and #2

1. Roll out the cookie dough. Cut the flamingo cookies with some facing in one direction and some facing in the other direction. Cut the heart cookies. Bake and cool the flamingo and heart cookies.

2. Fit a pastry bag with tip #2. Fill the bag with black run sugar icing. Outline the bird, bird details, and hearts using black run sugar icing. Allow the icing to set completely.

3. When the icing is firm, fill in the body outline with run sugar icing. Fill in the wing with run sugar icing. The left bird is pink with dark pink wings. The right bird is light pink with pink wings. Fill in the top of the beak with golden yellow run sugar icing. Fill in the bottom of the beak with black run sugar icing. Pipe the eye using black run sugar. Fit a pastry bag with tip #2. Fill the bag with pink soft peak royal icing. Pipe the flamingo legs. Fill in the heart outline with red run sugar icing.

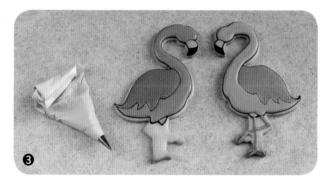

Pretty Peacocks

## Techniques

Trimming the Cut Cookie Dough
(pg. 118)

Combine Cookie Dough Shapes
(pg. 118)

Run Sugar Icing (pg. 126)

Detailed Piping with Royal Icing
(pg. 133)

## Materials

6-inch (15 cm) flamingo cookie
cutter

4½-inch (11.4 cm) oak leaf cookie
cutter

Mini pizza cutter

Run sugar icing: white, royal
blue, electric blue, green,
yellow, black

Royal icing, soft peak: black,
electric blue

Tips #1.5, #1, and #2

1. Roll out the cookie dough. Cut out one flamingo and one oak leaf for each peacock. Trim the flamingo leg so both legs will be standing. Trim the flamingo beak to be smaller. Cut a trapezoid shape for the peacock's head crest. Place the head

   crest on top of the head, slightly overlapping the trapezoid with the head. Press gently to connect. Place the oak leaf on the back of the flamingo for the peacock feathers, slightly overlapping the oak leaf and flamingo body. Press gently to connect. Bake and cool the peacock cookies.

2. For stability, turn over the cooled cookie and add royal icing to the seams where the crest joins the head and the tail joins the body.

3. Outline and fill the peacock wings with royal blue run sugar icing. Outline and fill one peacock feather with green run sugar icing. Pipe a dot with yellow run sugar icing. Place a toothpick in the center of the yellow dot and drag the toothpick to create a teardrop shape. Pipe an electric blue dot inside the center of the yellow dot. Place a toothpick just above the electric blue dot and

   drag through the yellow, stopping at the center. Lift the toothpick. Repeat with all the peacock feathers.

4. Pipe the white of the eye using white run sugar icing. Pipe the body using electric blue run sugar icing. Pipe the beak with black run sugar icing. Allow the peacock to set completely. When set, fit a pastry bag with tip #1.5. Fill the bag with black soft peak royal icing. Outline the peacock details. Fit a pastry bag with tip #1. Fill the bag with black soft peak royal icing. Pipe the peacock comb. Fit a pastry bag with tip #2. Fill the bag with black soft peak royal icing. Pipe the peacock legs. Fit a pastry bag with tip #2. Fill the bag with electric blue soft peak royal icing. Pipe dots on top of the black lines on the comb.

Circus Animals

## Techniques

Detailed Piping with Royal Icing
(pg. 133)

Run Sugar Icing (pg. 126)

## Materials

Circus tent cookie cutter and
embosser

Circus elephant cookie cutter
and embosser

Circus seal cookie cutter and
embosser

Circus clown cookie cutter and
embosser

Run sugar icing: white, red,
orange, yellow, green, blue,
light gray, light blue, light pink,
black

Tips #1.5 and #0

1. Roll out the cookie dough. Cut out the shapes using the circus cutters. Before baking, emboss the cut shape using the embosser. Bake and cool the embossed cookies.

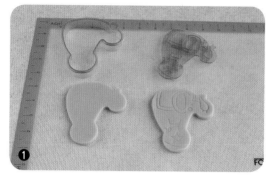

2. Fit a pastry bag with tip #1.5. Outline the details using black run sugar icing. Allow the black outline to set.

3. When the black outline is set, fill pastry bags with the colored run sugar icings. Fill in the details with the desired colors of run sugar icing. Use a toothpick to reach tight areas. Allow the icing to set. When set, pipe the elephant's eye, seal's eye, and clown's eyes with black run sugar icing. Fit a pastry bag with tip #0. Fill the bag with black run sugar icing. Pipe the clown's eye details.

Jungle Animals

## Techniques

Layer Baked Shapes (pg. 118)

Run Sugar Icing (pg. 126)

Detailed Piping with Royal Icing (pg. 133)

## Materials

Mix and match animal cookie cutter set

Run sugar icing: white, black, purple, light purple, blue, light blue, golden yellow, light golden yellow, brown, orange, light orange, gray

Royal icing: white

Royal icing, soft peak: black

Tip #1

# General Instructions

1. Bake and cool a head and a body for each animal. Outline and fill the body using run sugar icing, piping one back leg and one front leg. Allow the legs to set. When set, pipe the other back leg and other front leg. Outline and fill the head and ears using run sugar icing. Allow the head to set. When set, pipe the nose and mouth area. Pipe the inside of the ear.

2. When the face is completely set, pipe the eyes and nose using black run sugar icing. Fit a pastry bag with tip #1. Fill the bag with black soft peak royal icing. Pipe the mouth with black soft peak royal icing. When the body is completely set, add details such as cheetah spots, zebra stripes, and tiger stripes using run sugar icing. Allow the details to set.

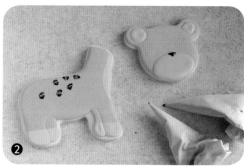

3. Spread white royal icing on the neck of the animal. Place the head on the body.

(CONTINUED)

# Zebra

Bake and cool a head and a body for the zebra. Outline and fill the body using white run sugar icing, piping one back leg and one front leg. Allow the legs to set. When set, pipe the tail, other back leg, and other front leg. Outline and fill the head and ears using white run sugar icing, leaving room for the nose. Outline and fill the nose with black run sugar icing. Allow the head to set. When the face is completely set, pipe the eyes, nostrils, and hair using black run sugar icing. When the body is completely set, pipe the zebra stripes and hooves using black run sugar icing. Use the same icing to pipe the end of the tail. Allow the details to set. Spread royal icing on the neck of the zebra. Place the head on the body.

> Place the head lower on the body for animals with SHORT NECKS, such as the hippopotamus. Place the head higher on the body for animals with LONG NECKS, such as the zebra.

# Hippopotamus

Bake and cool a head and a body for the hippopotamus. Outline and fill the body using purple run sugar icing, piping one back leg and one front leg. Allow the legs to set. When set, pipe the other back leg and other front leg. Outline and fill the face using purple run sugar icing. Allow the face to set. When the face is set, pipe the nose with light purple run sugar icing and pipe the ears with purple run sugar icing. Allow to set. Pipe the nostrils with purple run sugar icing. Pipe the eyes using black run sugar icing. Spread royal icing on the neck of the hippopotamus. Place the head on the body.

# Rhinoceros

Bake and cool a head and a body for the rhinoceros. Outline and fill the body using blue run sugar icing, piping one back leg and one front leg. Allow the legs to set. When set, pipe the other back leg and other front leg. Outline and fill the face using blue run sugar icing. Allow the face to set. When the face is set, pipe the nose with light blue run sugar icing and pipe the ears with blue run sugar icing. Allow to set. Pipe the nostrils with blue run sugar icing. Pipe the horn with white run sugar icing. Pipe the eyes using black run sugar icing. Spread royal icing on the neck of the rhinoceros. Place the head on the body.

# Cheetah

Bake and cool a head and a body for the cheetah. Outline and fill the body using golden yellow run sugar icing, piping one back leg and one front leg, leaving room for the feet. Allow the legs to set. When set, pipe the feet with light golden yellow run sugar icing. Allow to set. When set, pipe the other legs using golden yellow run sugar icing. Allow to set and pipe the remaining feet. Outline and fill the head and ears using golden yellow run sugar icing. Allow to set. When set, pipe the insides of the ears and the cheek area with light golden yellow run sugar icing. Allow the head to set. When the head is completely set, pipe the eyes and nose using black run sugar icing. Fit a pastry bag with tip #1. Fill the bag with black soft peak royal icing, and use it to pipe the mouth and the dots on the cheetah's cheeks. When the head and body are completely set, pipe the cheetah spots using brown and black run sugar icing. Allow the details to set. Spread royal icing on the neck of the cheetah. Place the head on the body.

> For SHORT, CHUBBY ANIMALS, such as the hippopotamus, pipe the back and front legs wide. For LEANER ANIMALS, such as the zebra, pipe the back and front legs thin.

# Tiger

Bake and cool a head and a body for the tiger. Outline and fill the body using orange run sugar icing, piping one back leg and one front leg. Allow the legs to set. When set, pipe the other legs. Outline and fill the insides of the tiger's ears and the center of the face using light orange run sugar icing. Outline the remaining part of the tiger's face and ears using orange run sugar icing. Allow the head to set. When the head is completely set, pipe the eyes and nose using black run sugar icing. Fit a pastry bag with tip #1. Fill the bag with black soft peak royal icing and pipe the mouth. When the head and body are completely set, pipe the tiger stripes using black run sugar icing. Allow the details to set. Spread royal icing on the neck of the tiger. Place the head on the body.

# Elephant

Bake and cool a head and a body for the elephant. Outline and fill the body using gray run sugar icing, piping one back leg and one front leg. Allow the legs to set. When set, pipe the other back leg and the other front leg. Outline and fill the face using gray run sugar icing. Allow the face to set. When the face is set, pipe the ear with gray run sugar icing. Pipe the eye using black run sugar icing. Fit a pastry bag with tip #1. Fill the bag with black soft peak royal icing and pipe the eyebrow with black soft peak royal icing. Spread royal icing on the neck of the elephant. Place the head on the body.

Regal Camels

## Techniques

Run Sugar Icing (pg. 126)

Detailed Piping with Royal Icing (pg. 133)

## Materials

5-inch (12.7 cm) camel cookie cutter

Run sugar icing: dark ivory, purple, deep pink, green, royal blue

Royal icing, soft peak: brown, golden yellow

Tip #1.5

Gold dusting powder

Grain alcohol

Fine brush

1. Bake and cool the camel cookies. Outline and fill the camel using dark ivory run sugar icing, leaving space for the blanket on his back and the bridle on his nose. Outline and fill the bridle and the blanket using purple, deep pink, green, or royal blue run sugar. Allow the camel, blanket,

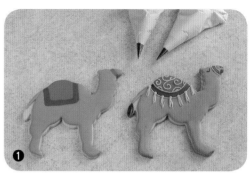

and bridle to completely set. When the camel is completely set, fit a pastry bag with tip #1.5. Fill the bag with brown soft peak royal icing. Pipe the end of the tail. Pipe the eye and the nostril. Fit another pastry bag with tip #1.5 and fill it with golden yellow soft peak royal icing. Outline and pipe details on the blanket and bridle. Allow the yellow to set completely.

2. When the golden yellow outline is completely set, mix the gold dusting powder with a small amount of grain alcohol, creating a paint. Paint the golden yellow outline with a fine brush.

Panda Bears

## Techniques

Layer Baked Shapes (pg. 118)

Run Sugar Icing (pg. 126)

## Materials

Mix and match animal cookie cutter set

Run sugar icing: white, black, and green

Royal icing: white

1. Bake and cool a head and a body for each panda bear. Outline and fill the belly on the body using white run sugar icing. Outline and fill the body with black run sugar icing, leaving room for the feet on the sitting panda. Allow the body to set. Outline and fill the face using white run sugar icing, leaving room for the eyes. Outline and fill the ears with black run sugar icing, leaving room for the inside of the ears. Outline and fill the eyes with black run sugar icing. Allow the head to set.

2. When the face is completely set, pipe the inside of the ears with white run sugar icing. Pipe the cheek area using white run sugar icing. Pipe a white dot for the eyes using white run sugar icing, then immediately pipe a smaller dot with black run sugar icing. Allow the cheek area to completely set, then pipe a nose using black run sugar icing. Pipe the feet on the sitting panda using white run sugar icing. Allow the feet to completely set, then pipe on the details of the feet using black run sugar icing. Pipe the arms with black run sugar icing. Spread royal icing on the neck of the animal and place the head on the body. Pipe bamboo on the sitting panda bear using green run sugar icing. Pipe the eye highlights using white run sugar icing.

Hungry Crocodiles

## Materials

7-inch (17.5 cm) crocodile cookie
cutter

2⅜-inch (6.1 cm) bird cookie
cutter

Run sugar icing: white, light
green, medium green, light
blue, light yellow, light pink,
orange

Royal icing, soft peak: brown,
light green

Tips #1 and #1.5

# Crocodile

1. Bake and cool the crocodile cookies. Outline and fill the crocodile shape with
light green run sugar icing, leaving the plates on his back, one front leg, and
one back leg uniced. Immediately add dots using light blue run sugar icing.
Allow the icing to set. When the icing is set, pipe the remaining front and back
leg using light green run sugar icing. Pipe the plates using medium green run
sugar icing. Fit a pastry bag with tip #1.5. Fill the bag with brown soft peak
royal icing and pipe two dots for the eyes using the brown soft peak royal
icing. Fit another pastry bag with tip #1.5. Fill the bag with light green soft
peak royal icing. Outline the eyes and pipe a mouth using the light green soft
peak royal icing. Pipe the teeth with white run sugar icing.

# Bird

2. Bake and cool the bird cookies. Outline and fill the bird body using light
yellow run sugar icing, leaving the wing uniced. Immediately add dots using
light blue run sugar icing. Immediately add the wing using light pink run sugar
icing. Pipe one tail feather. Allow the icing to set. When the icing is set, pipe
a second tail feather. Allow the icing to set. Pipe the third tail feather. Fit a
pastry bag with tip #1. Fill the bag with brown soft peak royal icing. Pipe the
legs and one dot for the eye using the brown soft peak royal icing. Pipe the
beak using orange run sugar icing.

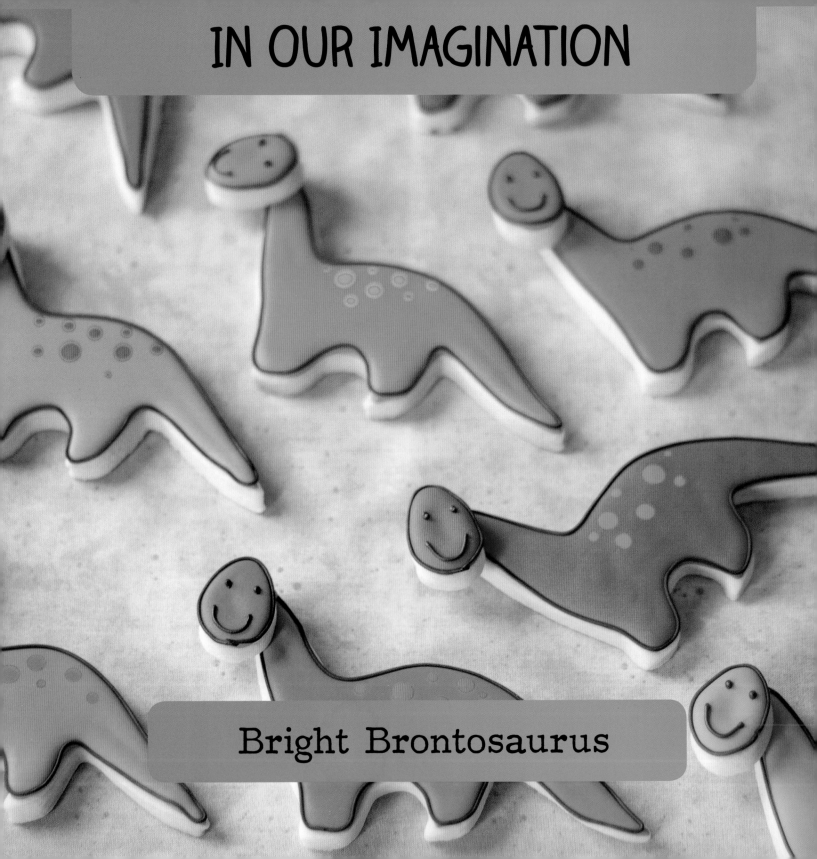

# IN OUR IMAGINATION

## Bright Brontosaurus

## Techniques

Layer Baked Shapes (pg. 118)

Run Sugar Icing (pg. 126)

Detailed Piping with Royal Icing (pg. 133)

## Materials

4½-inch (11.4 cm) brontosaurus cookie cutter

1⅜-inch (3.5 cm) egg cookie cutter

Run sugar icing: red, orange, electric blue, electric green

Royal icing, soft peak: black, white

Tip #1.5

1. Bake and cool the brontosaurus and egg cookies. Outline and fill the brontosaurus shape with run sugar icing. Immediately add dots using a contrasting color of run sugar icing. Allow the icing to set.

2. Outline and fill the egg shape with run sugar icing. Allow the icing to set. When the icing is firm on both shapes, fit a pastry bag with tip #1.5. Fill the bag with black soft peak royal icing. Outline the brontosaurus body

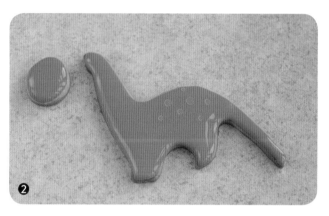

and the egg using black soft peak royal icing. Pipe a mouth and two dots for the eyes using the black soft peak royal icing. Attach the head (egg) to the body using white stiff peak royal icing.

Rainbow Unicorns

## Techniques

Rolled Fondant (pg. 137)

## Materials

5¼-inch (13.3 cm) unicorn cookie cutter

2-inch (5 cm) star cookie cutter

Star plunger cutters

Paring knife

Rolled fondant: white, purple, pink, orange, yellow, lime green, light blue, black, and green

Fondant extruder

Brush

Piping gel

Edible glitter or disco dust

# Unicorn

1. Bake and cool the unicorn cookies. Knead and soften white rolled fondant. Roll to 2 mm thickness. Cut the unicorn with the same cutter used in baking. Cut off the hooves, mane, horn, and tail. Brush piping gel onto the baked and cooled unicorn cookies. Place the fondant unicorn on the cookie. Emboss the unicorn's eye using the round end of a brush. Use a paring knife to carve a V in the eye for the eyelashes. Emboss the unicorn's mouth and nostril using the paring knife.

2. Knead and soften purple rolled fondant. Roll to 2 mm thickness. Cut the hooves using the unicorn cookie cutter. Place the hooves on the cookie.

3. Fit a fondant extruder with a disk that has multiple round openings. Form snakes of equal length and diameter with pink, orange, and yellow rolled fondant. Combine the snakes and feed the fondant extruder.

4. Extrude the fondant, cutting into small pieces after about 1 inch (2.5 cm) of extruding. Always make sure the disk is clean before extruding additional pieces.

5. Repeat steps 3 and 4 using yellow, lime green, and light blue fondant snakes. Brush piping gel onto the unicorn mane and tail. Add the extruded pieces to the unicorn, starting at the bottom of the tail first. Work your way up the tail. Next, start at the bottom of the mane, and work your way up the mane. Finally, add a couple of small pieces in front of the unicorn's ears.

6. Knead and soften black rolled fondant. Roll a small ball for the unicorn's eye. Knead and soften green rolled fondant. Roll a smaller ball for the inside of the unicorn's eye. Knead and soften white rolled fondant. Roll a tiny ball for the eye highlight. Attach the eye to the unicorn using piping gel. Roll white fondant to 2 mm thickness. Cut the unicorn horn. Place the horn on the cookie. Brush the horn with piping gel. Sprinkle with edible glitter or disco dust*.

7. Knead and soften rolled fondant of various colors. Roll thin. Cut and plunge stars. Attach to the unicorn with piping gel.

# Star

8. Bake and cool the star cookies. Knead and soften pink rolled fondant. Roll to 2 mm thickness. Cut the star with the same cutter used in baking. Brush piping gel onto the baked and cooled cookie. Place the cut fondant star on the cookie. Repeat with the other colors of rolled fondant.

\* If disco dust is used on the horn, remove the horn before eating cookie.

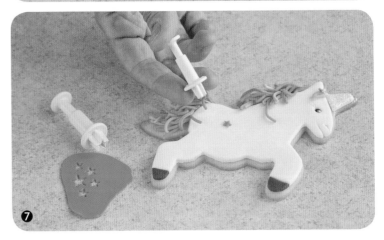

Dragons

## Techniques

Rolled Fondant (pg. 137)

## Materials

4½-inch (11.4 cm) standing dragon cookie cutter

5½-inch (14 cm) walking dragon cookie cutter

Mini football cookie cutter

Craft knife

Paring knife

Rolled fondant: white, green, light green, brown, blue, light blue, orange, light orange

CelPin or ball tool

Piping gel

# Standing Dragon

1. Bake and cool the standing dragon cookies. Brush piping gel onto the baked and cooled cookies. Knead and soften green rolled fondant. Roll to 2 mm thickness. Cut the dragon with the same cutter used in baking. Place the fondant dragon on the cookie.

2. Using a craft knife, cut the ears, wing, and belly off of the fondant. Cut a small notch in the tail. Cut into the mouth. Cut a jawline.

3. Use the CelPin and make an indention on the head for the dragon's horns. Knead and soften white rolled fondant. Form two small teardrop shapes. Emboss the teardrops using a paring knife. Knead and soften green rolled fondant. Roll a small ball. Indent the ball using the CelPin for the dragon's nostril. Knead and soften light green rolled fondant. Roll to 2 mm thickness. Cut the dragon with the same cutter used in baking. Using a craft knife, cut the belly and place it on the dragon cookie. Emboss the belly using the dull side of the paring knife. Cut the wing and place it on the dragon cookie.

4. Knead and soften green rolled fondant. Roll very thin. Using the standing dragon cookie cutter, cut the wing. Use a small football cutter to cut out the details in the wing. Using a craft knife, cut the leg and foot. Roll a snake. Bend the snake to form the arm. Cut the fingers using the craft knife. Knead and soften brown rolled fondant. Roll two balls for the eyes. Knead and soften white rolled fondant. Roll two small balls for the eye sparkle. Form two small teardrops for the toenails. Roll white fondant very thin. Cut two small triangles for the dragon's teeth. Attach the dragon's details using piping gel.

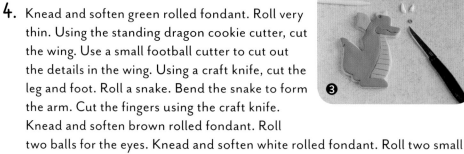

# Walking Dragon

1. Bake and cool the walking dragon cookies. Brush piping gel onto the baked and cooled cookies. Knead and soften blue rolled fondant. Roll to 2 mm thickness. Cut the dragon with the same cutter used in baking. Place the fondant dragon on the cookie.

2. Using a craft knife, cut the ears, wing, belly, and underside off of the fondant. Cut into the mouth. Cut a jawline.

3. Use the CelPin and make an indention on the head for the dragon's horns. Knead and soften white rolled fondant. Form two small teardrop shapes. Emboss the teardrops using a paring knife. Knead and soften blue rolled fondant. Roll a small ball. Indent the ball using the CelPin for the dragon's nostril. Knead and soften light blue rolled fondant. Roll to 2 mm thickness. Cut the dragon with the same cutter used in baking. Using a craft knife, cut apart the dragon. Cut the underside and the belly and place it on the dragon cookie. Emboss the underside and the belly using the dull side of the paring knife. Cut the wing and place it on the dragon cookie.

4. Knead and soften blue rolled fondant. Roll very thin. Using the walking dragon cookie cutter, cut the wing. Use a small football cutter to cut out the details in the wing. Knead and soften brown rolled fondant. Roll two balls for the eyes. Knead and soften white rolled fondant. Roll two small balls for the eye sparkle. Roll white fondant very thin. Cut two small triangles for the dragon's teeth. Attach the dragon's details using piping gel.

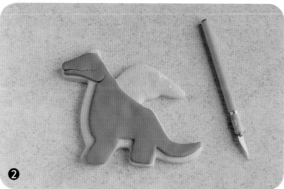

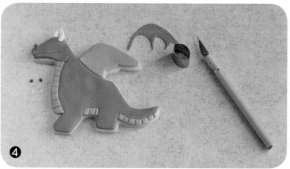

# BAKING AND DECORATING

## Tools for Baking

The following tools are useful for baking and decorating creature cookies. A rolling pin, a cookie sheet, a cooling rack, and cutters are the basic necessary tools. Other tools, such as perfection strips and flour shakers, are not essential, but make the rolling and cutting process more efficient.

## Cookie Sheets

Cookie sheets come in a variety of finishes, styles, and sizes. Choose a shiny, generously sized cookie sheet with no sides or one side. There should be at least 1 inch (2.5 cm) between the oven wall and cookie sheet for even heat circulation. A 14- by 20-inch (35.5 by 51 cm) cookie sheet fits in standard ovens while allowing enough air circulation. A cookie sheet with no sides or one side allows a cookie spatula to be easily slid under the cookie near the edges of the sheet. Cookie sheets with a dark finish tend to brown the bottoms of the cookies too quickly. It is handy to have two or three cookie sheets to keep the baking process efficient. Allow cookie sheets to cool before placing unbaked cookies on the sheet so the cookies do not spread.

## Rolling Pins

The two most popular styles of rolling pins for rolling cookie dough are classic rolling pins (with handles) and baker's rolling pins (without handles). Rolling pins with handles should have ball bearings for ease in rolling. I prefer a baker's rolling pin because it allows the weight to be distributed on the barrel, rather than the handles, which may cause fatigue in the hands and wrists. However, it takes a bit of practice to master rolling the cookie dough using a rolling pin without handles.

Choose a rolling pin that is wide enough to handle a large sheet of cookie dough. The more the cookie dough is rolled, the more overworked the dough becomes. Rolling pins with a small barrel may be easier to handle, but the dough will need to be rerolled several more times compared to a rolling pin with a longer barrel.

Rolling pins are made in a variety of materials. Wood and silicone are the most popular. Silicone rolling pins are ideal for rolling cookie dough because of the stick-resistant surface.

Some rolling pins come with rings that fit on each end of the barrel to assist in rolling the dough evenly. Rings can also be purchased separately to fit on barrels with specific diameters. Perfection strips are an alternative to rolling pin rings.

# Perfection Strips

For successful cutouts, the dough must be rolled perfectly even. Perfection strips come in sets with several different thicknesses. Place the cookie dough between two strips of the same size. Roll over the strips and the dough will be a consistent thickness. A rolling pin with rings can be used instead of perfection strips (see above).

# Flour Shaker

Flour shakers provide excellent control when dispersing flour onto the work surface or onto cookie dough.

# Silicone Baking Mats and Parchment Paper

To keep cookies from becoming too tough, avoid flouring the surface when rolling cookie dough. Parchment paper provides a nonstick surface for rolling dough. A silicone mat may also be used for rolling cookie dough; however, the mat may need a dusting of flour to prevent the dough from sticking.

Baked cookies will not stick when the cookie sheets are lined with parchment paper or a silicone mat. It is handy to have two or three silicone baking mats to keep the baking process efficient. Silicone mats and parchment paper cool quickly after they are removed from a hot cookie sheet. Allow the parchment paper or mat to cool completely before rolling dough or placing unbaked cookies on the mat.

Cookies can be rolled and baked on the same parchment paper or silicone mat. Roll the cookie dough and cut the shapes. Remove the excess dough, but leave the cut cookies in place. Slide the baking mat or parchment paper with the cut cookies onto a cookie sheet, and bake.

Silicone baking mats come in several sizes. Measure your cookie sheet and select a mat the same size as or slightly smaller than the cookie sheet. Parchment paper comes on a roll or in precut sheets. Parchment paper can be reused a few times during the same baking day.

# Cookie Spatula

A cookie spatula has a wide, thin blade to easily transfer cookies from the work surface to the cookie sheet and from the cookie sheets to cooling racks. Avoid using a narrow spatula that may not be wide enough to support the cookies.

# Cooling Rack

It is important to cool cookies on a cooling rack so they will have air circulation. Cookies that are left to cool on the counter may become soggy on the bottom. Choose a cooling rack with closely arranged wires in a grid pattern to prevent smaller cookies from slipping through. Stacking cooling racks are convenient when space is an issue.

# Cookie Cutters

Thousands of cookie cutter shapes are available in nearly every theme imaginable and in a variety of finishes, including copper, tinplate, plastic, plastic-coated metal, and stainless steel. Tinplate cutters are inexpensive and will bend easier than copper or stainless steel, but in most cases can be bent back to their original shape. Because tinplate is more flexible, cutters can be distorted to create a more desirable shape. Copper and stainless steel are more durable and will hold their shape after cutting dozens of cookies. Copper cutters most often are not as sharp as tinplate cutters. Take care when cleaning all metal cutters because they may rust or discolor if not thoroughly dried after washing. Plastic cutters or plastic-coated metal cutters are wonderful because they do not rust. Usually they are not as sharp, making them an obvious choice when cutting cookie dough shapes with children. If the shape desired is unavailable, there are even cookie cutter kits to create your own designs.

# Paring Knives

A paring knife is a must-have for removing excess cookie dough from cookies spaced tightly together or cookies with intricate details.

# Tools for Decorating

The type of icing used determines which decorating tools are required. Pastry bags and tips are used for run sugar or any icing that requires piping. Rolling pins, gum paste cutters, and extruders are used for rolled fondant-covered cookies.

## Stand Mixer

A stand mixer is helpful for mixing icings to the proper consistency. This can be exhausting if using a hand mixer.

## Pastry Bags and Parchment Cones

Several sizes and materials are available. Choose a reusable bag that is thin and lightweight and conforms to your hand when squeezed. Disposable bags are convenient for cleanup. A 12-inch (30.5 cm) disposable or reusable bag is a standard size for decorating. Smaller bags are easier to control, but they need to be refilled more often. Larger bags are more difficult to control, but they hold more icing. Use pastry bag ties or twist ties to keep icing from spilling out of the bag. Bag ties and twist ties are especially helpful when decorating cookies with kids.

A parchment triangle is used to form a cone to create a homemade disposable pastry bag. Simply remove the tip and toss the bag when you are finished decorating. Stands hold filled pastry bags and are also handy for filling pastry bags with icing, allowing both hands to be free. Tall drinking glasses can be used as well. Some pastry stands include a sponge on which the pastry tip rests. This keeps the icing in the tip from hardening.

## Pastry Tips and Couplers

A variety of pastry tips are used for many types of icings. Run sugar icing requires small, round-opening tips. It is handy to

have several of these tips so that you do not have to wash them constantly when piping different colors. PME Supatubes are superior to standard metal tips. They are stainless steel and seamless and have precise openings. The PME numbers vary slightly, but are close to standard tip numbers. Choose PME Supatubes #0, #1, #1.5, #2, #2.5, and #3. Buttercream icing will hold its shape when piped, and there are several tips to create fun piped designs. Tip #233, with its multiple small, round openings is ideal for fur or grass. A coupler is a two-part tool used when you want to change the tip and continue using the same pastry bag. A tip-cleaning brush is an invaluable tool. The small cylinder shape is designed to reach the hard-to-clean points of tips.

# Brushes

An assortment of round and flat brushes are useful for nearly all the icings in this book. Reserve a set of brushes to use exclusively with food. Brushes with round bristles that come to a fine taper are ideal for painting details on run sugar. Round brushes with large, soft bristles are used to apply dusting powders. Pastry brushes are used to apply piping gel onto cookies to attach rolled fondant.

# Rolled Fondant Cutters

Cut out decorations from rolled fondant with these special cutters. These cutters are typically smaller in size than cookie cutters, so they are excellent to use for small accents on iced cookies.

# Texture Mats and Texture Rolling Pins

Texture mats and texture rolling pins add an instant allover pattern to rolled fondant. Cookie cutters with coordinating texture mats are available for quick decorating.

# Spatulas

Cake decorating spatulas are used to mix and color icing. Spatulas used in cake decorating have a long, thin metal blade. Spatulas or palette knives with a thin, tapered blade are used for lifting rolled fondant accents and placing them onto the cookie.

# Toothpicks

Toothpicks are used to remove food color from jars. Always start with a clean toothpick when dipping into the jar. Reusing the toothpick may contaminate the food color in the jar. Toothpicks are also handy to coax icing into small areas.

# Scissors

A sharp pair of kitchen scissors is useful for trimming off the point on parchment bags to create tiny openings.

# Clay Gun or Fondant Extruder

These extruders are used to make rolled fondant lines and ropes with a consistent thickness. The extruder kits include a variety of interchangeable disks.

# Cutting Tools

The mini pizza cutter is a handy tool for trimming cookie dough. This tool is also invaluable when cutting strips and pieces of fondant. Use a stainless steel ruler to ensure cut strips are straight. The flexible, stainless steel fondant blade is thin enough to make micro-thin cuts without crushing the rolled fondant. A pair of small scissors can be is used for snipping small, precise cuts in fondant. A bench scraper is a tool with a large, flat blade and a handle for cutting through large chunks of fondant. The bench scraper is also handy for cleanup. Hold the blade at a 45-degree angle and scrape the work surface to remove crusted pieces of fondant.

# Modeling Tools

A set of modeling tools is essential for embossing fondant-covered cookies as well as other projects. A basic starter kit should include ball tools in a variety of sizes, a tool with a cone at the end, a veining tool, and a dog bone tool. Other practical tools include a quilting wheel, a shell tool, and scribing needle. CelSticks are handy modeling tools used for many applications. These sticks have a rounded end and a tapered, pointed end.

# Pasta Machine

A pasta machine for rolling fondant can be a costly investment, but it is very handy. They are available as freestanding machines or attachments for mixers, such as a KitchenAid. Generally, accents on cookies should be rolled very thin, such as setting #5 on a KitchenAid pasta attachment. Alternatively, roll fondant between two perfection strips of the same thickness. These strips will not roll fondant as thin as a pasta machine does, but they are useful for projects when a thin sheet is not necessary.

# Food Color and Edible Decorations

There are lots of edible decorations to give quick color and dimension to a cookie.

## Food Color

Gel, paste, powder, and liquid are the most common forms of food color. Gel and paste colors are the most popular. They are water-based and highly concentrated. Concentrated colors are the best to use because they will give the most vibrant color without affecting the consistency of the icing. Powdered food colors are also highly concentrated. It is best to dissolve the powdered granules before mixing the color into the icing; otherwise dark speckles may appear. Dissolve the powdered granules in a small amount of water before mixing the color with royal icing. For buttercream and rolled fondant, blend a small amount of vegetable shortening with the powdered color. Liquid color can be found in grocery stores and is best suited for pastel colors because dark colors are difficult to obtain. Too much liquid color may affect the consistency of the icing.

It is not necessary to have every color available. A cabinet full of icing colors can be overwhelming and messy, and take up a lot of space. Red, yellow, and blue are the only colors one needs to mix all other colors. However, it can be inconvenient and sometimes difficult to mix additional colors every time you need them. Keeping a jar of each of the primary colors (red, blue, and yellow) and secondary colors (purple, green, and orange)—as well as pink, black, ivory, and brown—will provide a nice assortment for nearly every color palette.

Deep shades such as red, black, purple, and royal blue darken as they set. If possible, mix these colors a shade lighter than desired the night before you need them; then check before use to see whether more color should be added. Darker colors may also make the icing bitter and leave a tinge on mouths when eaten. When mixing black or brown, cocoa powder can be added to the icing to obtain a deep shade with a pleasant taste before adding the color.

Keep decorated cookies covered or the colors may fade. Natural sunlight and fluorescent lights are the harshest on colored icings, but common household lighting may also cause colors to fade.

## Food Color Markers

Markers filled with food color are used to color details on any icing that forms a firm crust, such as rolled fondant or run sugar. Several companies manufacture markers in a wide spectrum of colors and tip sizes. It is handy to keep a set of fine-tip markers as well as markers that have a broad tip.

## Dusting Powders

Dusting powders can be brushed onto cookies for an allover application. Mix with grain alcohol to create a paint. Luster dusts, platinum dusts, and pearl dusts have a shimmer and are available in many metallic colors, including gold, silver, copper, and pearl. Super pearl is one of the most useful powders because it can be brushed onto any color to give a white-metallic sheen. It looks best when brushed onto cookies with white or pastel icings. Petal dusts have a matte finish and provide realistic shading.

## Sugars

Sugars add a sparkle when applied to cookie icings. Sanding sugar is coarser than granulated sugar and provides more sparkle. Coarse sugar is coarser than sanding sugar and may look heavy on small cookies.

# Edible Glitter and Edible Glitter Dust

Edible glitters are small, edible flakes that give a subtle sparkle under light. Edible glitter dust is an extra-fine powder, used for the same effect. Edible glitter and edible glitter dust do not add flavor or texture.

# Disco Dust

Disco dust, sometimes called fairy dust, provides the most sparkle; it is nontoxic, but not FDA approved. Disco dust should only be used for decoration and not eaten.

# Edible Round Candies

Round balls of sugar in a variety of colors and sizes provide instant dimension and color. Nonpareils are tiny balls typically used as an allover application on a cookie. For smaller animal cookies, black nonpareils are perfect for eyes. Sugar pearls or candy beads range in size from 2 to 7 mm. These pearls are ideal to use as eyes on larger animal cookies. Sixlets are larger, approximately 10 mm in size. Nonpareils, sugar pearls, and candy beads are sugar-sweetened balls with a hard shell. Sixlets have chocolate inside with a candy shell. Some of the round candies are available with a pearl finish, giving a subtle sheen.

# Piping Gel

Piping gel is a clear, flavorless gel used to attach edible decorations to cookies. Decorations can be placed on the cookie while the icing is wet, or piping gel may be used as a glue to attach the decorations after the icing dries. Piping gel is also brushed onto baked cookies to attach rolled fondant. Piping gel comes in a tub or a squeeze tube.

# Cookie Recipes

All of the cookies in this book were made using one of the two recipes that follow: a basic sugar cookie recipe and a chocolate cookie recipe. Both recipes provide a cookie with simple, subtle sweetness that is enhanced with icing. When mixing the dough, a stand mixer with a flat beater attachment is ideal, but a hand mixer may be used. These cookies will hold their shape when baked, which is especially important for cookies covered with rolled fondant. If using a recipe not included in this book, eliminate any leavening agents to prevent the cookies from spreading. The yield amounts given are approximate, as the number of cookies baked is determined by their thickness and the size of the cutters. Baked cookies, with or without icing, taste best when eaten within seven to ten days.

## Buttery Sugar Cookies

This recipe is simple to mix and rolls and freezes beautifully. It is very important to chill the dough to firm the cream cheese and butter. If this dough is rolled immediately after mixing, additional flour may be needed when rolling, which will toughen the dough. Use cream cheese in block form. Cream cheese in a tub has added ingredients that may cause the cookie dough to be extra sticky. The flavor can be altered by replacing the vanilla with other extracts. Some of my favorite replacements are orange and lemon. If I replace the vanilla with a different extract, I often add the same extract in my icing to enhance the flavor.

*1 cup (225 g) unsalted butter, softened*

*3 ounces (85 g) cream cheese, softened*

*¾ cup (170 g) sugar*

*1 teaspoon (5 ml) vanilla extract*

*1 egg*

*3 cups (330 g) all-purpose flour*

1. Mix the butter and cream cheese in an electric mixer on medium speed for 2 to 3 minutes, or until blended. Scrape down the sides of the bowl.

2. Add the sugar. Continue to blend on medium speed until the mixture is light and fluffy. Mix in the vanilla.

3. Add the egg, mixing on low until thoroughly blended. Scrape down the sides of the bowl.

4. Add the flour, 1 cup (110 g) at a time. Scrape the bowl after adding each cup. Mix until just incorporated. Do not overmix or the dough will toughen.

5. Divide the dough into two equal portions. Flatten the dough into two patties that are approximately 1 ½ inches (3.8 cm) thick. Wrap the patties with plastic wrap and refrigerate for at least 2 hours, or until firm.

6. Preheat the oven to 375° (190°C, or gas mark 5). Bake the cookies for 9 to 11 minutes, or until the edges are very lightly browned.

*Yield: Thirty-six 3- to 4-inch (7.5 to 10.2 cm) cookies*

# Chocolate Cookies

These delicious chocolate sugar cookies have a flavor similar to a brownie. The type of cocoa powder used will change the flavor and color of the cookie. Dutch-process cocoa powder tends to have a richer color and flavor. Replace the vanilla extract with peppermint or mocha extract for a fun twist on a classic chocolate cookie. After mixing the dough, it is ready to use immediately. This cookie dough tends to be a bit more crumbly than the Buttery Sugar Cookie dough when rolling. These cookies can easily be overcooked because it is difficult to know when they are done, as the edges do not brown. If they are overbaked, they become very crisp.

3 cups (330 g) all-purpose flour

⅔ cup (75 g) unsweetened cocoa powder

½ teaspoon salt

1 cup (225 g) unsalted butter, softened

1½ cups (340 g) sugar

2 eggs

2 teaspoons (10 ml) vanilla extract

1. In a large bowl, blend the flour, cocoa powder, and salt.

2. Mix the butter and sugar in an electric mixer on medium speed for 2 to 3 minutes, or until light and fluffy. Scrape down the sides of the bowl.

3. Add the eggs and vanilla, and mix on low speed until thoroughly blended. Scrape down the sides of the bowl.

4. Add the flour mixture, 1 cup (110 g) at a time. Scrape the bowl after adding each cup. Mix until just incorporated. Do not overmix or the dough will toughen.

5. Divide the dough into two equal portions. Flatten the dough into two patties that are approximately 1 ½ inches (3.8 cm) thick. Use the dough immediately, or place the dough in the refrigerator until ready to mold or roll.

6. 6. Preheat the oven to 350° (180°C, or gas mark 4). Bake the cookies for 8 to 10 minutes, or until no indentation is made when touched.

Yield: Thirty-six 3 to 4-inch (7.5 to 10.2 cm) cookies

## Important Tips

• Always use high-quality ingredients. Butter is superior to margarine. Using low-fat ingredients may produce cookies that are better for you but will compromise the taste and baking properties. Allow refrigerated ingredients such as butter or cream cheese 30 minutes to an hour to come to room temperature before mixing.

• It is important to properly measure when mixing dough. Not enough flour can make the dough difficult and sticky to roll; too much flour will cause the cookie to be tough and dry. When measuring flour, scoop the flour into the measuring cup so that the flour is overflowing. Use the straight edge of a knife or spatula to scrape off the excess flour.

• If a baked cookie breaks, repair it with royal icing. When decorating, the icing will cover up the crack.

• If the dough cracks or breaks when rolling, the dough is likely too cold to roll. Allow the dough to come to room temperature. If the dough is sticking, it did not chill long enough in the refrigerator or it has gotten warm as it has been rolled. Too much cream cheese or butter may also cause sticking. Place the dough in the refrigerator for an hour or two. If the dough is still sticking, dust the work surface and the top of the cookie dough with a bit of flour.

## Storing Cookie Dough

Mixed cookie dough can be stored in the refrigerator for up to a week. After mixing the cookie dough, flatten the dough into a large circular patty about 1 ½ inches (3.8 cm) thick. Tightly wrap with plastic wrap and place in the refrigerator. Allow the dough to come to nearly room temperature before rolling. Both of the cookie dough recipes in this book freeze well. The dough can be kept for up to three months in the freezer. Wrap the cookie dough with two or three layers of plastic wrap. Wrap again with a layer of foil. When ready to thaw, place the frozen dough in the refrigerator for several hours. Allow the dough to come to nearly room temperature before rolling or molding.

## Shelf Life of Baked Cookies

Generally, cut-out cookie recipes have a longer shelf life than most baked goods. I prefer to have my cookies eaten within seven to ten days, but most cut-out cookies will keep for up to three weeks. The icing recipes included in this book will keep for several weeks at room temperature. It is the baked cookie, not the icing, that determines the shelf life. Refrigerating the decorated cookie may cause the icing colors to bleed or have spots. Follow the instructions for storing decorated cookies according to each icing recipe for best results.

## Freezing Baked Cookies

Cookies that are cut out and baked freeze beautifully. Decorated cookies, on the other hand, do not freeze well. Colors bleed or spotting occurs. To freeze undecorated cookies, allow the baked cookies to cool completely. Place the cookies in a single layer in a box. Place a sheet of parchment paper on top of the first layer. Add more cookies in single layers until you reach the top of the box. Close the box. Tightly wrap the box with two or three layers of plastic wrap, then wrap with a layer of foil. Place the sealed box in the freezer. Remove the box from the freezer several hours before the cookies will be decorated, and place it on the counter. Do not remove the plastic wrap or foil until the cookies have come to room temperature. Once the cookies have thawed and are at room temperature, they are ready to decorate.

# Rolling Cookie Dough and Cutting Shapes

To achieve a cookie with perfect thickness, use perfection strips or use a rolling pin with rings. Some rolling pins include rings, while others are sold separately. If purchasing the rings separately, make sure to measure the size of the rolling pin barrel beforehand. The rings will only work with rolling pins with a specific diameter, which varies depending on the brand. The type of icing to be used determines which size of perfection strips or rolling pin rings to use. Cookies with a thin layer of icing can be rolled to 4 mm. Cookies with a heavy amount of icing, such as buttercream, are best rolled at 6 mm. Most of the cookies in the book were rolled at 4 mm or 6 mm.

With the following technique of rolling dough, the cookie dough is rolled on a silicone mat or sheet of parchment paper. After the dough is rolled, the shapes are cut and the excess dough is removed, leaving the cut shaped untouched. The advantage to this method is that you will have perfectly shaped cookies with no distortion.

1. Start with dough that is chilled. Place the cookie dough on a silicone mat or a sheet of parchment paper. Center the dough between two perfection strips. Roll over the strips, leveling the cookie dough.

2. Use a cookie cutter to cut shapes. The shapes should be spaced approximately ¼ inch (6 mm) apart. The cookie recipes in this book hold their shape, so they can be cut very close together, eliminating excessive working of the dough.

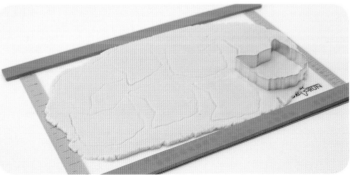

**3.** Remove the excess dough using a paring knife. The scraps can be rerolled and used to cut more shapes.

**4.** Slide the parchment paper or silicone mat onto a cookie sheet. Bake the cookies according to the recipe instructions. After the cookies are baked, allow the cut shapes to cool for 3 to 4 minutes. Use a cookie spatula to gently transfer the warm cut shapes to a cooling rack. Baked cookies will be fragile and soft to the touch while they are still hot. Take extra care when moving the baked cookie from the cookie sheet to the cooling rack. Allow the cookies to cool completely before decorating.

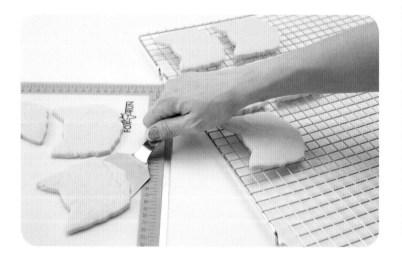

## Important Tips

• Cookie dough may not release from cookie cutters with thin or highly detailed shapes. If part of the cookie dough remains in the cutter while part of the cookie dough releases, dip the cookie cutter in flour before cutting the next shape. Cutters may be stretched and reshaped slightly if necessary to get the dough to release from a tight area.

• Chill the cookie dough if the recipe requires chilling. It is frustrating to try to roll soft cookie dough. The dough may be sticky, and cut-out shapes will be difficult to remove. If the dough is still sticking after chilling, it can help to dust a small amount of flour on the silicone mat, parchment paper, or work surface and on top of the cookie dough.

• Cookie dough becomes overworked if the dough is rolled over and over. The less the dough is rolled, the better. Overworked dough will cause the cookie to become very dry and tough. Dough that has been rolled over and over may also produce cookies with a distorted or shrunken shape. For best results, mix the dough and divide it into two patties. After cutting shapes from the first patty, set the scraps aside. Roll and cut shapes from the second patty, and set the scraps aside. Combine the scraps from both patties and roll. Repeat until there are no remaining scraps. The best shaped cookies will come from the first batches of rolled dough.

• For best results, cut out shapes that are consistent in size for even baking. Cookies bake best on the center rack of the oven and when one cookie sheet is used. If two cookie sheets are used, space the oven racks evenly in the oven and rotate the two cookie sheets every 4 to 5 minutes to encourage even baking.

• Transfer baked cookies from hot cookie sheets to a cooling rack soon after the cookies are out of the oven to prevent them from browning any further. If the cookies are on a parchment sheet or silicone mat, the sheet or mat can be slid onto the cooling rack. If the cookie sheet is not lined with parchment paper or a silicone baking mat, the baked cookies may stick if left on a hot cookie sheet too long.

# Cookies on a Stick

Create cookie pops or baked cookies on a stick to assemble lovely edible arrangements. When baking cookies on a stick, the cookies must be firm after they are baked or they will break off the stick. To ensure a firm cookie, cool the cookies on a rack so the bottom does not become soft or soggy. Do not underbake the cookies. It is better to have the edges browned slightly than to have a cookie that is too soft. The cookie recipes included in this book are ideal to use for cookies on a stick. Use long, paper sticks. Plastic sticks may melt in the oven and are not recommended. Paper sticks may brown slightly, but that's okay; you can wrap them with bright ribbons, if desired. Wooden sticks may be used, but they are more difficult to trim.

1. Follow the directions for rolling cookie dough on page 115 and cut out the shapes desired. To insert a stick, press the end of the stick into the dough from the bottom. The end that is inserted into the base of the cookie dough should be resting on the cookie sheet. Hold the other end of the stick between your index finger and thumb. With your dominate hand, begin twisting the stick and pushing the stick up into the cut cookie dough shape. Keep the stick as parallel to the cookie sheet as possible. Use the index finger of your nondominant hand to keep the stick from protruding through the cookie dough. Continue twisting and pushing until the stick is approximately three-fourths through the cut shape.

## Important Tips

• It is important to keep in mind the position of the shapes when cutting cookie dough for cookies on a stick. Make sure there is plenty of room for the sticks to protrude from each cut shape. It is also important to consider placement of the sticks. Your oven may not have ample room for sticks placed in every direction.

• If the cookie becomes loose from the stick after baking, add a bit of royal icing or chocolate to the back of the cookie, securing the stick.

# Designing and Planning Your Cookie Creature

It is important to plan your baking and decorating. Use the time management suggestions along with the shelf life and storage recommendations to guide your planning. Spending a few minutes planning can save hours of frustration. The first step is to design the shape of your finished cookie; then plan the decorating process.

Cookie cutters come in hundreds of shapes and designs. Many cutters are designed to have a realistic effect. I tend to choose whimsical designs. If you can't find a cutter that you like, use the following ideas to customize the cutter or modify the cookie dough. Another option is a cookie cutter kit. This kit lets you make your own cutters. However, if just a few custom-shape cookies are needed, a pattern made from cardstock (instructions follow) may be a more practical option.

## Trimming the Cut Cookie Dough

Cut the shape and then use additional cutters, a knife, or a mini pizza cutter to remove unwanted cookie dough. For the hamster cookies, a frog cutter and a mini pizza cutter were used. First the frog is cut; then the mini pizza cutter is used to remove the legs of the frog, creating a chubby hamster.

## Stretch the Cookie Cutter

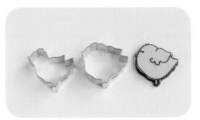

Adjust the shape of the cutter by stretching and pulling the metal. This gives the creatures a chubby, whimsical effect. The chick cutter on the left is the original cutter. The cutter was stretched to create a pudgy chick.

## Layer Baked Shapes

Bake and decorate shapes, then stack them to create a fun layered cookie. The polar bear uses a bear head cookie cutter with a snow globe cookie cutter for the body.

## Combine Cookie Dough Shapes

Cut shapes and piece them together to form your own designs. For the stacked turtle cookies, three separate cutters were used. Cut the three shapes. Arrange the shapes as desired, overlapping the edges. Gently press the cookie dough together to combine the shapes and eliminate the seams. After the cookie is baked, it may be necessary to reinforce the delicate seam on the back with royal icing.

## Make Cardstock Patterns

Draw or trace the shape desired onto a sheet of cardstock. Then cut out the shape. Spray the back of the cardstock with cooking spray. Place the greased side of the cardstock on the rolled cookie dough. Use a mini pizza cutter to cut as much as possible, giving the cleanest edge. Use a paring knife to cut any corners. Remove the excess dough. Round any corners by gently pressing on them with your index finger.

## Designing the Colors and Details

Before decorating the cookie, it is a good idea to plan the inside design. Place the cookie cutter on a sheet of paper. Outline the cookie cutter (or baked cookie)

with a pencil. Draw the design inside the outline. The Internet can also be helpful when planning the inside design of the outlined shape. For example, when decorating an outline of a sitting bunny, you may have difficulty visualizing where the legs extend. Type "sitting bunny clipart" in your browser and view the resulting images for ideas. For additional visualization, the drawing can be colored. Coloring may be extra work that may not be necessary, but it provides a visual of all the colors that will be used. There have been many times that I have discarded colored icing, only to find that I needed the color later! If I don't take the time to color with colored pencils, I write down the colors needed for each cookie.

## Time Management

When decorating cookies, it is most efficient to decorate in an assembly line. Decorate the same detail on each of the cookies before moving to the next detail. This will make the decorating process faster and allow time for the first detail to dry or crust before adding the adjoining detail. When planning the baking and decorating process, it is important to allow enough time for the dough to chill, the baked cookies to cool, and the decorated cookies to dry. This means that although it can be done, baking and decorating may not be a one-day process. If the cookies will need to be packaged, allow the cookies to set loosely covered for at least a day before packaging. Humid areas may require longer drying times.

## Storing Decorated Cookies

Keep decorated cookies in a loosely covered container or a cake box that is not airtight. Containers that are airtight may cause the cookie to have trapped moisture, resulting in spotting or stickiness on the cookie surface.

## Shelf Life of Decorated Cookies

Generally, it is the baked cookie, not the icing used, that determines the shelf life of the cookie. A baked cookie taste best when eaten within seven to ten days.

## Freezing Decorated Cookies

Humidity is the main deterrent when freezing cookies. Moisture may cause colors in the run sugar to bleed or develop tiny moisture spots. Rolled fondant–covered cookies may also spot with the presence of moisture. Baked cookies that are not decorated freeze beautifully. Allow the frozen cookies to come to room temperature before decorating. If baked cookies or decorated cookies must be frozen ahead of time, be sure to follow the direction on page 114.

# Using Pastry Bags and Parchment Cones

A pastry bag or a parchment cone holds the icing as you decorate. A pastry bag or parchment cone will conform to your hand, making it easy to control the flow of icing for piped designs. A parchment bag is made by shaping a parchment triangle into a cone. Tips may be dropped into the parchment bags or pastry bags without a coupler, or a coupler may be used to change tips without filling a new bag. Cleanup is easier using a parchment cone or disposable pastry bag. Simply snip off the end of the bag, remove the tip, and discard the bag. You only need to clean the tip.

## Fitting a Bag with a Coupler

1. Cut the reusable pastry bag or disposable pastry bag so that one or two threads are showing on the coupler base when it is dropped into the bag. Pull the coupler tightly to secure.

2. Place the tip on the coupler base.

3. Twist the coupler screw top to tighten the tip in place.

# Using a Bag without a Coupler

1. A tip can be dropped into a bag without a coupler. Cut the bag so that the bottom third of the tip protrudes from the pastry bag.

~~~~~~~~~~~~~~~~~~~~~~~~~~~~~~~~~~~~~

## Important Tips

• Each time pastry bags are refilled, there is a buildup of air. Before beginning to pipe again, squeeze the pastry bag to release trapped air; otherwise, a large air bubble will interrupt the piping.

# Filling Reusable and Disposable Pastry Bags

1. Drop the tip into the pastry bag and tug on the end to secure. The bag may also be fitted with a coupler following the instructions above. Fold the pastry bag over your hand to form a cuff 2 to 3 inches (7.5 cm) long. For ease in filling, the bag can be placed in a tall drinking glass or a pastry bag holder with the cuff folded over.

2. Scoop icing into the bag until it reaches the top of the cuff, or until the bag is about half full with icing. The fuller the bag, the more difficult it is to control.

3. Unfold the cuff. Squeeze the bag between your thumb and fingers, and push the icing toward the bottom of the bag.

4. Twist the bag where the icing begins. For more security, secure with a rubber band, twist tie, or icing bag tie to prevent the icing from bursting from the top of the bag.

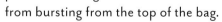

# Making a Parchment Cone

Parchment paper is available in precut triangles. These triangles are formed to create pastry bags that are lightweight, inexpensive, and disposable. If a parchment cone is well made, a tip may not be needed when a round opening is desired. Simply cut the tapered end of the parchment cone to the size needed.

1. The triangle is labeled A, B, and C.

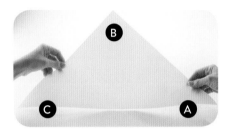

2. Fold corner A to meet corner B, twisting to form a cone.

3. Fold corner C to meet corner B, keeping the cone shape with a tight point. Align all three points.

4. Cross over corners A and C, making a "W" to overlap the seams. Always keep the bottom point tight. Shift A and C up and down to ensure a tight point.

5. Fold in the corners of the bag to secure, or secure the seam with tape.

6. Cut the parchment bag at the point, large enough so one-third of the tip will protrude from the bag.

7. Drop the tip, narrow end first, into the bag. If more than one-third of the tip is showing, the tip may pop out of the bag during piping.

# Filling Parchment Cones

**1.** Hold the parchment bag and fill halfway with icing.

**2.** Squeeze the bag between your thumb and fingers to fill the bottom of the bag.

**3.** Fold in the left side, then the right side. Fold down the middle, and continue to fold until you reach the top of the icing.

# Holding the Bag

**1.** Throughout the book, the directions will instruct you to hold the pastry bag at various angles. The most common angles are 45 and 90 degrees. To control the icing, grip the bag with your dominant hand. Use the tip of the index finger of your nondominant hand to guide the bag. Squeeze the icing while guiding the bag.

## Important Tips

• The seam of the parchment bag can be secured with tape if it is difficult to maintain a fine point while filling the bag.

## Important Tips

• If not covered, tips in filled pastry bags that are sitting unused will likely become clogged with hardened or crusted icing. Keep the filled pastry bags covered with a damp cloth or a tip cover when not in use.

# Royal Icing

Royal icing is most commonly used for three purposes in cookie decorating. The first and most common use is to thin with water to create a glaze called run sugar or flood icing. Adding water to royal icing provides a sweet, firm icing that dries with a hard finish but will not be difficult to bite into. The second use of royal icing is to pipe outlines and designs. The third use is as a glue when assembling houses, creating layered cookies, or making other three-dimensional cookie projects.

The royal icing recipes in this book yield a stiff, fluffy icing. Use either of the following two recipes. A commercial royal icing mix is also available for convenience. Simply add water to the powdered mix and beat on high speed for several minutes. Mixing bowls and utensils should be spotless and grease-free. Grease will make the royal icing break down, causing the cookies to become spotted. Use a damp cloth to cover bowls of royal icing and the tips of filled pastry bags when not in use to prevent the icing from drying out. Royal icing mixed from egg whites should be used within the day. Royal icing made with meringue powder or prepared with a commercial royal icing mix can be stored in an airtight container for several days. Refrigerating the icing will extend the shelf life for up to two weeks. The icing consistency will likely change as it sits. Water may evaporate, causing the icing to become stiffer. Royal icing may also separate. It is important to thoroughly mix royal icing or run sugar just before using to ensure the proper consistency. If the icing is too stiff, add a small amount of water. When piping fine details with a #2 tip or smaller, it is best to use fresh (just mixed) royal icing. Any powdered ingredients, including the powdered royal icing mix, should be sifted before mixing.

Royal icing has a subtle sweetness. Flavoring can be added for extra taste. Blend the flavoring in by hand, adding a small amount at a time until the desired taste is obtained. Water- or alcohol-based flavors are best to use when flavoring royal icing. After royal icing is mixed, add the color and/or flavor. If water will be added to the royal icing, add the color and flavor to the icing before adding the water. If the flavor or color has thinned the royal icing, add powdered sugar to thicken the icing.

## ROYAL ICING WITH MERINGUE POWDER

4 tablespoons (60 ml) meringue powder

½ teaspoon cream of tartar

⅔ cup (160 ml) water

8 cups (888 g) powdered sugar, sifted

1 tablespoon (15 ml) gum arabic

In a mixing bowl, combine the meringue powder, cream of tartar, and water. Beat on high speed until stiff peaks form. In a separate bowl, stir together the powdered sugar and gum arabic. Mix thoroughly and add to the meringue. Beat on low speed until incorporated, then mix on high speed for several minutes until stiff peaks form. Keep the icing covered with a damp towel.

*Yield: 4¾ cups (1.2 L)*

## ROYAL ICING WITH EGG WHITE

1 pound (454 g) powdered sugar

3 large egg whites, at room temperature

⅛ teaspoon cream of tartar

Sift the powdered sugar. Pour the egg whites into a mixing bowl. Mix in the cream of tartar and powdered sugar. After all the ingredients are incorporated, beat on high speed until stiff peaks form. Keep the icing covered with a damp towel.

*Yield: 2½ cups (625 ml)*

### Important Tips

• To eliminate the risk of salmonella, dried egg whites may be used. Dried egg whites are reconstituted with a small amount of water. Purchase dried egg whites at cake decorating supply stores.

# Royal Icing Consistencies

The following pictures show how royal icing consistency is good for some techniques but too thick or too thin for others. The same tools are used in each picture. A spatula spreads the icing at the far left. The swirl designs are piped using tip #1. The hearts are outlined and filled using tip #1. The drop flowers are piped using tip #22. When adding water, blend the water by hand to avoid incorporating extra air.

Piping royal icing with a soft peak is also easier on the hands. To obtain a soft peak, add a small amount of water to the stiff royal icing after it is whipped. The amount of water needed will vary. Start with approximately ½ teaspoon of water, then add a few drops at a time until the peak is fluffy, soft, and curved. The peak should not stand upright. Royal icing with a stiff or soft peak should not flow from the bag without squeezing.

## THICK CONSISTENCY (STIFF AND SOFT PEAK)

Royal icing with a soft peak is used in many of the cookies throughout this book, especially for piping outlines or fine details. Stiff or soft peak royal icing is too  thick for filling in outlines (shown on the heart). When the royal icing is made with one of the two recipes above, it will have a stiff peak. Royal icing with a stiff peak is often used in cake decorating, but in this book, I use royal icing with a soft peak because the stiff peak tends to chip off the cookie.

## MEDIUM CONSISTENCY

Run sugar icing, or royal icing with a medium consistency, is a smooth icing that flows when piped onto cookies. This consistency is used for glazing cookies and should not  be used for fine lines and details because lines will go flat and details will be lost. Mix royal icing according to the recipe until stiff peaks form, then add drops of water to achieve a medium consistency. Royal icing with a medium consistency should flow from the bag with light squeezing. For more information on run sugar icing, see the following chapter.

# Run Sugar Icing

Run sugar icing is the most commonly used icing for cookies. For years, run sugar-iced cookies have adorned countless magazine covers. Run sugar icing is created by thinning fluffy, stiff royal icing to create a glaze, or icing that flows. This icing has a subtle sweetness that is not overpowering. It dries with a matte, hard surface and will have a bit of crunch when bitten. Because this icing dries hard, these decorated cookies are good for stacking and shipping. Allow the cookies to dry for several hours or overnight before packaging or stacking them.

Keep icing bowls covered with a damp cloth to prevent the run sugar from forming a crust. Run sugar in bowls or pastry bags should be fine for a few hours, but the icing tends to thicken as water evaporates. Run sugar may also separate. If the icing thickens or separates, remove the icing from the bag, stir, and add water if necessary. Keep the tips covered with a damp cloth. When done for the day, squeeze the leftover icing from the bags into bowls. Cover the bowls with an airtight lid for up to a week. Place tightly covered run sugar in the refrigerator to extend the shelf life for up to two weeks.

After the cookies are decorated, keep them on the work surface or place them on a cookie sheet or tray to dry for several hours. Moving the cookies while they are drying may cause the cookies to have tiny cracks on the surface. If the cookies are placed on a tray to dry, use as little movement as possible while moving the tray.

## Thinning Royal Icing to Create Run Sugar

To create run sugar, simply add water to royal icing. Gently fold the water into the icing by hand. Whipping the icing too vigorously or using a mixer will incorporate too much air, causing air bubbles on the decorated cookies. Add enough water to the royal icing so that when piping, the icing will smooth itself in 7 to 10 seconds. Run sugar should be about the consistency of honey. Each mixed batch of royal icing will vary in viscosity, so the amount of water added may vary from batch to batch.

This icing can be used to outline and then immediately fill in to create a decorated cookie without a strong, visible border. The outline can also be piped and then filled in with a contrasting color of icing. The outline and fill should be the same consistency. Some decorators prefer to outline the cookie in a stiff icing and fill in the outline with a thinner icing. I prefer to use the same thickness. This requires less effort when mixing and cleaning; plus bleeding may occur if the outline and fill icings are not the same consistency.

1. Mix royal icing according to the recipe directions. The royal icing should be stiff. Add food color if desired.

2. Add a few drops of water to the royal icing and gently fold. Add more drops of water until the royal icing is similar in consistency to honey. Spoon a small amount onto parchment paper.

3. Drag a knife through the center. The icing should hold its shape, but smooth back together within 7 to 10 seconds. If the icing is too thick, it will remain separated. Add more water and repeat the test. If the icing is too thin, it will create a larger puddle and will smooth together quickly. More icing or powdered sugar can be added to thicken it.

4. Once the icing is the correct consistency, spoon it into a pastry bag. A pastry bag holder (shown) is ideal to keep the icing bag upright when filling. A tall drinking glass may also be used. After the bag is filled, fold the corners (see page 120 for pastry bags and parchment cones). If the icing flows from the pastry bag without squeezing, it is too thin.

## Important Tips

· Use bowls with squared edges or bowls with a spout for ease in filling squeeze bottles and pastry bags.

# Outlining Cookies

Outlining is the first step when decorating with run sugar. Determine if a visible or invisible outline is desired. The visible outline is often black or brown. This gives the cookie a fun, coloring book effect. The invisible outline gives a softer appearance and is generally less time consuming.

## Choosing the Right Decorating Tip for Outlining

The size of the cookie should determine which decorating tip to use. Use these guidelines for most decorating. For the most precise outline and fine details, use a decorating tip.

Cookies smaller than 2" (5 cm): Tip #1 (red) or #1.5 (orange)

Cookies 2 to 3" (5 to 7.6 cm): Tip #1.5 (orange) or #2 (yellow)

Cookies 3 to 4" (7.6 to 10.2 cm): Tip #2 (yellow) or #3 (green)

Cookies 4 to 6" (10.2 to 15.2 cm): Tip #3 (green) or #4 (blue)

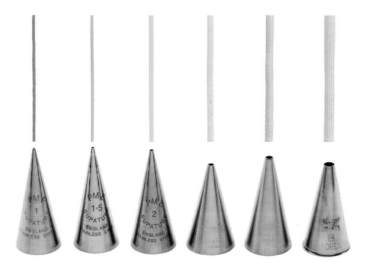

## Visible Outline

1. Fit a pastry bag with a small, round opening such as tip #1.5 or #2. Fill the pastry bag with run sugar icing. Hold the bag at a 45-degree angle with your dominant hand. Use the index finger of your nondominant hand to guide the bag. Touch the cookie with the piping tip to attach the icing. After the icing has attached to the cookie, continue squeezing and lift the icing, so that the pastry tip is slightly raised above the cookie while outlining. Touch the cookie to guide the end of the outline and attach the icing. It also may be necessary to touch the cookie when piping sharp corners.

2. Outline any additional areas. Allow the outlines to dry for several minutes.

3. With run sugar in a contrasting color, fill a pastry bag fit with a round opening such as #3 or #4, or cut a hole at the point of a parchment cone. Follow the original outline using the contrasting color of run sugar, piping a second outline. Fill in the contrasting outline. Do not leave any area uniced, or the icing may come together on its own, trapping air and causing the iced cookie to have unsightly craters.

4. Use a toothpick to spread icing into sharp angles. A toothpick can also be used to remove tiny air bubbles that may have risen to the surface immediately after filling in the outline.

5. Fill in additional colors. Use a toothpick as described above.

6. If fine details are desired, allow the cookie to dry for several hours. Pipe additional details, referring to "Detailed Piping with Royal Icing" on page 133. Allow the cookies to dry for several additional hours or overnight before packaging or stacking them.

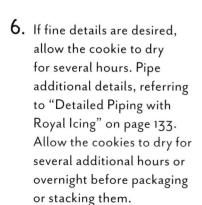

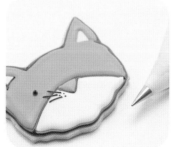

## Important Tips

• If the icing is not smooth, and the piping lines are visible after filling in the outline, the icing is too thick. The icing may be helped along by resting the iced cookie in the palm of your hand. Tap the back of your palm gently on the work surface to smooth the cookie. If there are still wrinkles, remove the icing from the pastry bag and blend the icing with a few drops of water before decorating the next cookie.

• When filling in an outline, a parchment cone with a hole cut in the corner works well instead of using a tip. This eliminates washing tips. It is also easier to unclog a bag with a cut hole instead of a tip. Use tip #3 if using a tip, or cut the parchment cone to size #3 for filling in outlines on smaller cookies. Tip #4 or #5 is better for filling in outlines on larger cookies.

• Another option is to follow the subsequent instructions for decorating a cookie using run sugar with no visible outline. Using that method, an outline can be added after the cookie is decorated. The difference is that when outlining first and then filling in the outline, the outline is made with run sugar. If decorating the cookie with run sugar, then outlining after, the outline is made with royal icing with a soft peak. See "Detailed Piping with Royal Icing" on page 133.

# Invisible Outline

1. Fit a pastry bag with a small, round opening such as #1.5 or #2, or use a parchment cone with a small hole cut in the corner. Fill the pastry bag with run sugar icing. Hold the  bag at a 45-degree angle with your dominant hand. Use the index finger of your nondominant hand to guide the bag. Touch the cookie with the piping tip to attach the icing. After the icing has attached to the cookie, continue squeezing and lift the icing so that the pastry tip is slightly raised above the cookie while outlining. Touch the cookie to guide the end of the outline. The tip should only touch the cookie to attach the icing and when ending the outline. Fill in the outline. Do not leave any area uniced, or the icing may come together on its own, trapping air and causing the iced cookie to have unsightly craters.

2. Add an adjoining color.

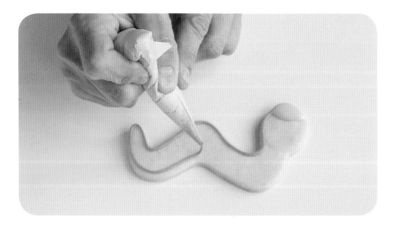

3. Fill in the adjoining color.

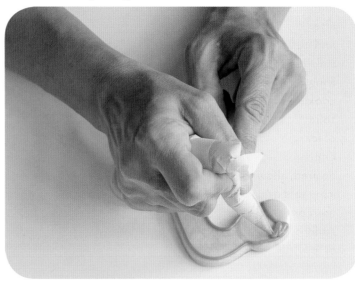

4. If the icing isn't smoothing, place the cookie in your palm and gently tap the back of your hand against the work surface.

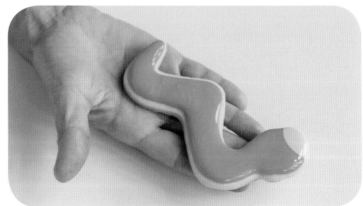

**5.** Details added immediately after outlining and filling will sink into the icing. This gives a cookie with one solid, flat piece of icing. If added dimension is desired, allow the icing to dry for an

hour or two before piping details. For more information on adding fine details, see "Detailed Piping with Royal Icing" on page 133. Allow the cookie2 to dry for several more hours or overnight before packaging or stacking them.

## Important Tips

• Use a toothpick to spread icing into sharp angles. A toothpick can also be used to remove tiny air bubbles that may have risen to the surface immediately after filling in the outline.

• To create definition without changing color, pipe small areas at a time and allow each area to harden before moving on to the next.

• When the area hardens, pipe the adjoining area. This will give the cookie an outline with dimension without piping.

# Storing Run Sugar-Iced Cookies

The run sugar–decorated cookies can be arranged on a serving plate or placed in cellophane bags after the run sugar has completely dried (allow at least 24 hours).

If the decorated cookies will not be served within a day, place them in an airtight container for up to ten days. The cookies can be stacked in the container, with parchment paper sheets in between each layer.

# Troubleshooting

- **The cookies are spotted.** Over time, the fats in the cookie may begin to break down the run sugar, which causes unsightly grease spots. Cookie recipes that have a high amount of fat, such as a shortbread, may cause grease spots. The recipes in this book are ideal for run sugar. Humidity may also cause spotting. Cookies decorated with run sugar are not well suited to freezing.

- **The icing is cracked.** Moving the iced cookie while the run sugar is drying may cause the cookie to have tiny cracks on the surface. Leave the cookies on the work surface and allow several hours to dry. If the cookies are placed on a tray to dry, use as little movement as possible while moving the tray.

- **The icing has tiny air bubbles.** Tiny air bubbles may surface after the cookie is iced. Use a toothpick to remove any air bubbles before the icing dries. Bubbles may be caused if too much air is incorporated when thinning royal icing to create the run sugar. Royal icing should be mixed in a mixer; but when adding water to the royal icing to thin, blend by hand. Run sugar icing that is too thin may contain more air bubbles.

- **The icing has small craters.** When filling in an outline, do not leave any area uniced, or the icing may come together on its own, trapping air. This will cause the icing to burst with small craters.

- **There are colored streaks** in the smooth icing. Streaks are caused by food color that is not thoroughly mixed.

- **The icing is bumpy.** The icing is too thick. Add more water. Taking too much time to fill in the outlined cookie may also cause bumpy icing.

- **The icing is falling off the cookie.** The icing is too thin. Add more royal icing or powdered sugar to thicken. Piping the outline too close to the edge may also cause the icing to fall off the cookie.

- **The icing has puddles.** Small water puddles may occur if the icing inside the pastry bag has separated. Run sugar icing in a pastry bag should be good for a couple of hours. Icing that will not be used for 4 hours or more should be removed from the pastry bag and placed in an airtight container. Stir the icing before filling a bag.

- **The colors are bleeding.** When dark or intense colors are next to one another, they may bleed. To avoid this, make sure the two icing colors are the same consistency. This should prevent bleeding. If bleeding still occurs, allow one color to dry for several hours before adding the adjoining color. Humidity and moisture may also cause the colors to bleed.

- **The accent piping is not detailed.** Allow each layer to dry before adding any details. Make sure the run sugar icing is not too thin.

# Detailed Piping with Royal Icing

Delicate royal icing details can be piped onto rolled fondant-covered cookies or run sugar-iced cookies using piping tips with small round openings, such as #0, #1, #1.5, #2, and #2.5. Before piping details onto a cookie iced with run sugar, allow the icing to set completely to prevent the details from spreading or sinking into the icing.

The consistency for piping is very important. Royal icing should be thick and fairly stiff with a soft peak, and should not flow from the tip unless the bag is gently squeezed. If the icing is too stiff, it may be difficult to squeeze the bag. If the icing is too thin, the details may become flat and undefined. Thoroughly sift powdered ingredients before mixing royal icing, because even the tiniest clump can clog the tip or cause icing to release in messy spurts.

Do not get discouraged if your cookies do not look perfect. It takes practice to master the flow, pressure, and consistency of the icing.

1. Fit a pastry bag with a small, round-opening tip. Fill the pastry bag with royal icing of medium consistency. Touch the iced cookie with the tip and squeeze the bag to attach the icing.

2. While still squeezing, lift the pastry bag and begin piping the details. Continue with steady pressure. Touch the surface and stop squeezing to attach the end of the detail.

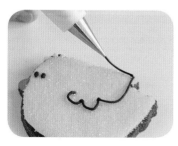

## Dots

Add a little water to the royal icing to obtain a medium to thick consistency—thinner than the royal icing used for piping details, but slightly thicker than icing used for run sugar. Holding the pastry bag at a 90-degree angle, apply a small burst of pressure to release icing. Stop the pressure, then lift. For very tiny dots, use minimal pressure. If the icing is too thin, the dots will lose dimension. If the icing is too thick, dots will have peaks. To soften peaks, dampen your index finger with water and gently press the peaks.

### Important Tip

• Apply gentle, consistent pressure while moving your hand across the cookie. If the royal icing lines are wiggly, you are applying too much pressure or moving too slowly. If the lines are breaking, you aren't applying enough pressure.

# Painted Cookies

A white run sugar-iced cookie or white rolled fondant-covered cookie provides the perfect canvas to create edible, painted works of art. Although it may sound intimidating to paint details, it is quite easy because the cookie cutter provides a nice outline and guide. Food color markers or food color gels thinned with water provide the coloring. Each gives a unique look. Food color markers are similar to coloring markers and provide a vivid, strong contrast with little shading. They are ideal for children to use and are handy for outlining or drawing fine details. These markers are available from several companies. Americolor has markers in bright vivid colors, while FooDoodler offers several sizes of tip openings. Food color gels thinned with water are similar to watercolor paints and give a more artistic appearance. Adding various amounts of water to the gel lets you create many shades. Note that liquid food colors do not provide enough concentration to create strong contrasts.

1. Cover the cookie with white rolled fondant following the instructions on page 138 or ice the cookie with white run sugar following the instructions of page 130. Allow the cookies to crust for 24 hours before painting.

2. Fill each cavity of a paint tray half full with water. Squirt small amounts of food color gel onto the top of the paint tray. Blend some of the food color gel with the water in the cavities to achieve a soft shade. Test the color on a white sheet of paper.

3. Outline any details with a very light shade of the color desired. Decide which areas will remain white, and outline with the color that will be surrounding the white area. For example, the mouse shown here will be painted gray, but the area around his eye will remain white.

**4.** Paint the cookie using a very light shade of the desired color. Leave a thin white line in between adjoining colors to keep them from bleeding into one another.

**5.** Blend the concentrated food color on the top of the paint tray with a small amount of water to create a thick, darker color for shading. Test the color on a white sheet of paper. Use the shading color to add contrast and shading to the cookie.

**6.** Allow the painted cookie to dry for several hours. Outline the cookie using a fine brush with concentrated food color, or use food color markers with a fine tip.

## Important Tips

• Make sure the brush is damp with the food color paint and not dripping with water. Too much water on the brush will cause the sugar to dissolve in the rolled fondant or run sugar icing. This will produce dark spotting or tiny air bubbles. Tiny air bubbles may also appear if the cookie was covered with run sugar icing that was too thin.

• A marker can be an efficient method for outlining. The rolled fondant must have several hours or overnight to crust, or the marker will indent the fondant when coloring. The run sugar icing must also have several hours or overnight to dry, or the markers will poke through the icing.

# Storing Painted Run Sugar-Iced Cookies

The run sugar-painted cookies can be arranged on a serving plate or placed in cellophane bags after the painting has completely dried (allow at least 6 hours). If the food color was not thinned with water, the painted cookie may remain sticky and leave a residue in the cellophane bags.

If the decorated cookies will not be served within a day, place them in an airtight container for up to ten days. The cookies can be stacked in the container, with parchment paper in between each layer.

# Buttercream Icing

There is no other icing like buttercream. This sweet, fluffy icing can be spread onto cookies or piped using various tips. Make buttercream following the recipe, or purchase it premade from cake and candy supply stores.

Buttercream icing forms a crust but remains soft and creamy on the inside. The icing may not crust in geographical areas that are humid. Colored buttercream may darken as the color sets, especially with deep colors such as red, emerald green, navy, purple, or black. Blend the color a shade lighter than the desired color. Wait for a few hours, then check. If the icing is too light, add more food color. If the icing is too dark, add more white buttercream.

When piping the icing onto the cookies, start with extra thick cookies or the sweetness from the icing will overpower the cookie. Buttercream is a basic, sweet icing that can be modified with a variety of flavors. Substitute the almond flavor with any extract. Popular extracts are peppermint, lemon, coconut, and coffee. Extracts and flavorings will vary in potency. Add to taste. Some flavors contain color, which may affect the tinge of the icing.

*½ cup (120 g) high-ratio shortening*

*4 cups (520 g) powdered sugar, sifted*

*5 tablespoons (75 ml) water*

*½ teaspoon salt*

*1 teaspoon (5 ml) vanilla flavoring*

*½ teaspoon almond flavoring*

*¼ teaspoon butter flavoring*

In a large bowl, combine all the ingredients; beat on low speed until well blended. Continue beating on low speed for 10 minutes or until very creamy. Keep the bowl covered to prevent the icing from drying out. Unused icing can be kept in the refrigerator for up to six weeks. Rewhip on low speed before piping.

*Yield: 4 cups (1 L)*

## Important Tips

• For bright white icing, use clear flavorings. Pure vanilla will give the icing an ivory hue.

• High ratio shortening is a baker's quality shortening produced to replace butter. It gives the icing a fine, smooth, and creamy texture without a greasy aftertaste. Solid vegetable shortening can be substituted for high ratio shortening. However, it will likely affect the icing consistency, texture, and flavor.

• Do not whip the icing on medium or high speed. Extra air will be incorporated, causing air bubbles. Whipping the buttercream on low speed creates a smooth and creamy icing.

• Food color in buttercream icing may deepen upon setting. Allow the icing to set for 2 to 3 hours to see true color.

• Delicious chocolate buttercream icing can be made by adding approximately 1 cup (112 g) of cocoa powder to the buttercream recipe. The cocoa powder may cause the buttercream to stiffen. Add a small amount of water to achieve the desired consistency.

# Rolled Fondant

Rolled fondant is rolled, cut, and placed on the cookie for an icing with a smooth, clean finish. Similar to working with clay or sculpting dough, rolled fondant can be sculpted, cut, or textured. It is commonly used as a sweet decorative covering on a cake.

However, rolled fondant serves as a wonderful sweet complement to cut-out cookies. It is important that the rolled fondant is about half as thick as the baked cookie or it will overpower the cookie. A recipe is included for those who wish to make rolled fondant from scratch. It can be time-consuming and difficult to make rolled fondant, so before attempting the recipe, purchase commercial rolled fondant so that you will be familiar with the proper texture. Though commercial rolled fondant varies in texture and flavor, it will help you get a feel for the outcome you want to achieve in your homemade version. It is also available in white or colors. If rolled fondant is overworked or if it seems dry, it will be stiff and tough. A touch of shortening or egg white can be added to soften the fondant. To color rolled fondant, simply add food color to the fondant and knead until there are no streaks of color. Excess color may cause the fondant to become sticky. Extra powdered sugar can be added to help with stickiness.

*½ cup (120 g) heavy cream*

*2 tablespoons (30 g) unflavored gelatin*

*¾ cup (270 g) glucose*

*2 tablespoons (28 g) butter*

*2 tablespoons (25 ml) glycerin*

*2 teaspoons (10 ml) clear vanilla flavor*

*2 teaspoons (10 ml) clear butter flavor*

*1 teaspoon (5 ml) clear almond flavor*

*Approximately 9 cups (1 kg) powdered sugar*

*Vegetable shortening*

1. Pour the cream into a small saucepan. Sprinkle the gelatin on top and cook over low heat until dissolved. Add the glucose, butter, glycerin, and flavorings. Heat until the butter is melted. Set aside.

2. Sift the powdered sugar. Place 7 cups (770 g) of the powdered sugar in the bowl of a stand mixer fitted with the dough hook. Pour the cream mixture over the powdered sugar and mix slowly until thoroughly combined.

3. Add the remaining 2 cups (220 g) powdered sugar and mix to combine. The fondant will be very sticky, but should hold its shape.

4. Lay a sheet of plastic wrap on the counter. Coat with a thin layer of vegetable shortening. Wrap the fondant in the greased plastic wrap and allow to set for 24 hours. After 24 hours, the fondant should be less sticky. If the fondant is still sticky, add more powdered sugar.

*Yield: 4 cups (1 L)*

# Covering a Cookie with Rolled Fondant

**1.** Brush a thin layer of piping gel onto a baked and cooled cookie. A few cookies may be brushed at a time with the piping gel, but the gel will dry as it sets if too much time passes.

**2.** Knead and soften the rolled fondant. Lightly dust the work surface with powdered sugar to prevent sticking. Place

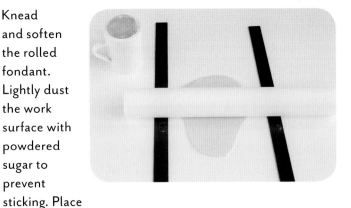

the rolled fondant on the dusted surface between two perfection strips, 2 mm thick. Roll over the strips, thinning the rolled fondant into an even sheet. A rolling pin with rings may be used in place of the perfection strips. When rolling, lift and turn the rolled fondant a quarter turn. Do not turn the rolled fondant over. If the rolled fondant is sticking while lifting and turning, dust with additional powdered sugar or knead powdered sugar into the rolled fondant to stiffen. Keep the top of the rolled fondant free of powdered sugar, or the covered cookie will have white spots or a white powdery finish.

**3.** Cut the rolled fondant with the same cutter used in baking.

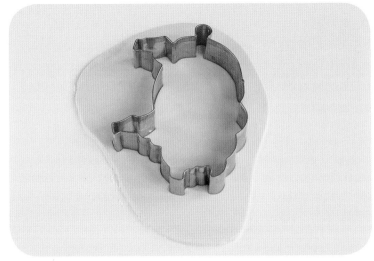

**4.** Lift the shape and place on the cookie brushed with piping gel.

# Embossing Rolled Fondant

**1.** Use the blunt edge of a paring knife to sculpt lines into the soft rolled fondant.

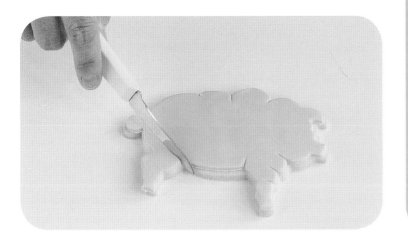

**Important Tip**

• Buttercream icing can be used in place of piping gel for additional sweetness. Pipe buttercream icing onto the cookie using tip #6, leaving approximately ½ inch (1.3 cm) uniced all along the outer edges of the cookie. Use a spatula with a thin blade to smooth the buttercream, taking care not to spread the icing off the cookie. Place the rolled fondant on top of the buttercream-iced cookie.

**2.** A tip with a round opening—or the bottom of a tip—can be used to emboss a U-shape. The U-shape is perfect for eyebrows, closed eyes, smiley faces, or frowns.

**3.** Press into the soft rolled fondant using a ball tool for round indentions. Round indentions are ideal for making crevices for eyes, ears, or polka dots.

# Pieced Rolled Fondant Cookies

**1.** Follow steps 1 through 3 for Covering a Cookie with Rolled Fondant.

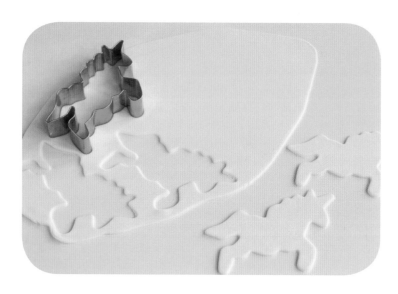

**2.** Using a mini pizza cutter or paring knife, cut any area that should be a different color. A paring knife is used to cut small areas.

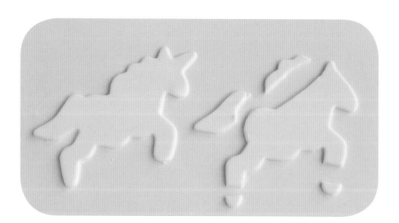

**3.** Place the cut piece on the cookie brushed with piping gel.

**4.** With a contrasting color of rolled fondant, follow steps 1 through 3 for Covering a Cookie with Rolled Fondant. Use the paring knife to cut the shape into pieces. Place the cut fondant on the cookie and piece together.

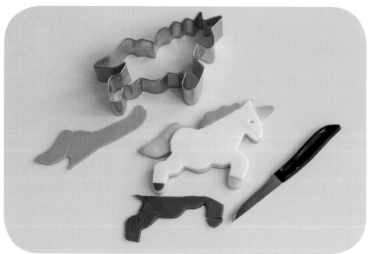

# Rolled Fondant Accents

Rolled fondant accents can be applied on nearly any cookie icing, including buttercream, run sugar, or rolled fondant-covered cookies. It is important to roll the fondant thin (approximately 1 to 2 mm) both for a dainty look and to prevent the texture and sweetness of the fondant accent from overpowering the baked cookie. Piping gel is used to attach the accents. Accents can be made several weeks ahead of time. Allow the accents to harden overnight, then place in a loosely covered box.

## Plunger Cutter

1. Knead and soften rolled fondant. Lightly dust the work surface with cornstarch. Roll the fondant thin. Holding the plunger by the base, cut the shape. Before lifting, gently wiggle to clean the edges.

2. Lift the cutter. Run your thumb over the edges to ensure a clean cut. Press the plunger to release the shape. Attach to the cookie using piping gel.

## Ribbon Cutter

1. Knead and soften rolled fondant. Dust the work surface with cornstarch. Roll the fondant thin. Rub the ribbon cutter with a thin layer of solid vegetable shortening. Cut the strips. Attach to the cookie with piping gel.

## Clay Gun or Fondant Extruder

1. Knead and soften rolled fondant. Roll a cylinder of fondant the length of the extruder and slightly smaller in diameter than the barrel. Feed it into the extruder from the bottom. Attach the desired disk to the extruder. Twist the handle to release the fondant.

2. Use a paring knife or a spatula with a thin blade to cut the extruded fondant. Attach to the cookie using piping gel.

## Mini Accent Cutters

1. Knead and soften rolled fondant. Dust the work surface with cornstarch. Roll the fondant thin. Cut the accents. Attach to the cookie with piping.

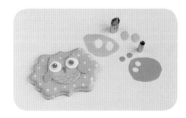

# Shading Iced Cookies

Colored powders are used to shade run sugar-iced or rolled fondant cookies. Pink dusting powder is practical to keep on hand to add rosy cheeks to your animals. These powders can be blended to create gradations of color. Color can be brushed onto rolled fondant as soon as the cookie is covered. If the cookie is iced in run sugar, allow the icing to dry completely before brushing on color. Petal dust provides a matte finish. Luster dust gives a shimmery finish. See page 110 and 111 for more information on dusting powders.

**1.** Ice the cookies with run sugar or rolled fondant. If using run sugar, allow it to set completely. Place the cookie on a sheet of parchment before brushing to collect excess dust.

**3.** To blend colors, brush in a circular motion where the colors meet.

**2.** Brush the powder generously onto the area of the cookie that will be shaded. Shown is red petal dust dusted onto the geckos.

**4.** Repeat with additional colors, if desired.

# Edible Frosting Sheets

Edible frosting sheets are pictures printed onto edible paper with food color. These sheets are easily applied and are one of the simplest techniques to quickly decorate a cookie using rolled fondant.

Edible sheets come in full sheets designs, side designs, and even designs to coordinate with some cutters. Full sheet designs approximately 8 by 10 inches (20 by 25 cm) will cover several 2- to 3-inch (5 to 7.5 cm) cookies. The side designs work for small cookies, or for adding sections of patterns on large cookies. The side designs are typically in strips that are 2½ inches (6.4 cm) wide by 10 inches (25 cm) long. When using any of the frosting sheets, be sure to use white rolled fondant, because it will not affect the color of the edible print. For example, if a design is applied to a cookie covered with pink rolled fondant, all white areas of the design may turn pink. It is important to store edible frosting sheets properly. Keep the frosting sheets tightly sealed in a plastic bag at room temperature. If the edible frosting sheets are difficult to remove from the paper backing, place in the freezer for 2 minutes.

1. Roll enough white rolled fondant to fit the frosting sheet, rolling to a 2 mm thickness. Remove the frosting sheet from the paper backing.

2. Turn over the frosting sheet. Brush the back of the frosting sheet with a thin layer of piping gel.

3. Place the frosting sheet on the rolled fondant. Gently roll over the fondant with minimal pressure to attach completely.

4. To eliminate wasting the nonpatterned rolled fondant, use a pizza cutter to remove excess fondant that extends past the frosting sheet and wrap tightly.

5. Brush the baked and cooled cookie with piping gel. Use the same cutter used in baking to cut the patterned fondant. Gently lift the cut shapes and place on the piping gel–coated cookies. Take care when lifting the pieces, as the frosting sheet may wrinkle.

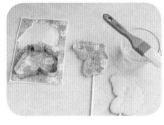

Frosting sheets are available to coordinate with some cookie cutters.

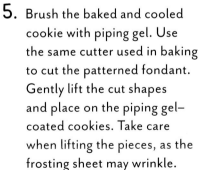

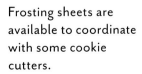

# Resources

## Online Shopping

**Autumn Carpenter Designs**

*www.autumncarpenter.com*

Mini accent cutters, perfection strips, texture mats.

**Country Kitchen SweetArt**

*www.shopcountrykitchen.com*

A one-stop shop carrying the cake and candy supplies used throughout the book.

**Sweet Elite Tools**

*www.sweetelitetools.com*

Cutters, texture mats.

## Blog

*www.autumncarpenter.wordpress.com*

## Websites

*www.autumncarpenter.com*
*www.cookiedecorating.com*

# About the Author

Autumn Carpenter's passion for decorating started at a very young age. Growing up in the confectionary industry, Autumn found joy in every aspect of the business. Autumn is co-owner of Country Kitchen SweetArt, a retail cake and candy supply store that has been owned and operated within Autumn's family for more than fifty years. The business caters to walk-in store sales, catalog sales, and online sales at www.shopcountrykitchen.com.

Autumn has demonstrated throughout the country, teaches on Craftsy.com, and serves as a judge in cake decorating competitions. She has been a member, teacher, and demonstrator at the International Cake Exploration Society (ICES) for twenty years.

Autumn's own line of useful tools and equipment for cake and cookie decorating can be found online as well as in many cake and candy supply stores throughout the United States and in several countries. She has written several books, including *The Complete Photo Guide to Cake Decorating; The Complete Photo Guide to Cookie Decorating; The Complete Photo Guide to Candy Making, Decorate Cakes, Cupcakes, and Cookies with Kids;* and *Let's Make Angry Birds[TM] Cakes.*

# Acknowledgments

Thanks once again to the best editor, Linda Neubauer, for the suggestion of writing an animal cookie book! Thank you to my kids—Isaac, Austin, Sydney, and Simon—who always make me smile and were understanding when I was decorating cookies instead of cooking dinner. Above all, I want to thank my husband, Bruce, who constantly stands beside me when I work on books and throughout my career.